THE

GREAT FRENCH REVOLUTION,

1785—1793.

NARRATED IN THE LETTERS OF MADAME J——,
OF THE JACOBIN PARTY.

EDITED BY HER GRANDSON, M. EDOUARD LOCKROY.

FROM THE FRENCH,

BY

MISS MARTIN, AND AN AMERICAN COLLABORATEUR.

London:

SAMPSON LOW, MARSTON, SEARLE, & RIVINGTON,

CROWN BUILDINGS, 188, FLEET STREET.

1881.

PREFACE BY THE TRANSLATORS.

THE remarkable letters that compose this volume form the only personal narrative that has been presented to the public by an eye-witness of the terrible events which they describe, from the revolutionary point of view. History and Memoirs have dealt with the Jacobin party and the popular cause, with advocacy and sympathy; but the well-known personal narratives are all on the other side, they are protests by the victims of the great convulsion. The unique character of the letters of Madame J——, the view which they present of the intellectual tastes and affectations of the period, and the curious evidence they afford of the irresistible carrying away of minds not naturally unreasonable or passionate, in the flood of that furious and phenomenal time, lead us to believe that this work will be interesting to English readers.

PREFACE BY THE EDITOR.

~~~~~~~~~~

MADEMOISELLE D——, my great grandmother, the daughter of a merchant at Pontoise, married, in 1774, Monsieur J—— (de la Drôme). They lived in retirement in a distant part of Dauphiné, near Romans, until 1785, when M. J—— took his eldest son to Paris, where the boy was to make his classical studies. His wife, after having remained for some time at Romans, with her youngest child, rejoined her husband and son in Paris, and there the Revolution overtook her. She was present at the meeting of the States-General, and at the great events of that epoch, events in which her husband was soon to be personally concerned.

When the Constituent Assembly had voted its own dissolution, M. J—— left Paris for Dauphiné. There he was nominated 'deputy supplementary' to the Legislative Assembly. He seems to have passed almost the whole of the time during which he held that deputyship at Romans, where he was detained both by political interests and family affairs. His wife wrote to him nearly every day, and she also wrote almost as frequently to her eldest son, who had been sent to London to finish his education. At a later period, M. J——, who was named deputy to the Convention, returned to Paris. Madame J—— continued to write to her son while he remained in England, and when he went to Toulouse, whither he was sent by the Government of the Republic, on a political mission. Of those letters this volume is composed.

Madame J—— did not think that her correspondence would ever be published. She did not write for the public, but for her own people. Having remained alone at Paris, she wanted to keep them informed of everything remarkable and important that occurred. For them she frequented the Jacobin's Club, the Tuileries Gardens, the Legislative Assembly; for them she made summaries of the speeches, described *fêtes* or risings, and took a part in the popular movements. Otherwise she led an austere life, receiving no one, and having for her sole associate an old servant named Marion, who aided her in bringing up her youngest child, who was always an invalid. Her letters have the charm of familiar talk. While she is relating the events of the day, she asks advice from her husband, and bestows it on her son. She imparts to them her hopes and her fears.   She mingles politics with her family affairs, and does all this with perfect simplicity, because she is speaking only to those who know and love her.

She married late.   At the time when she wrote these letters she was between forty and forty-five years of age.   She was a highly educated woman; thoroughly acquainted with classical literature, and she knew the Latin, Italian, and English languages. Her style reveals the influence of Rousseau and the great writers of the eighteenth century; it does not, however, lack individuality.   It is that of a worthy woman, and of a passionately fond mother, who narrates all that she sees, with the emotion of the actual moment, and who, having nothing to conceal, speaks with perfect liberty and open-heartedness.   All her letters, and a household. account-book, two extracts from which are given in the notes to this volume, have come into my hands with other family papers.   I have scrupulously respected the text, and I have admitted a few letters written by her husband, which I found among the others.   Lastly, I have not suppressed the first part of the correspondence, which dates from 1785, and has no reference to political events.   All this portion—it is very brief—seemed to me to possess interest as a picture of the happy and simple life of a family, about to take a part in the great revolu-

tionary convulsion, in their country home. This
short prelude was requisite to introduce the writer
of these letters to the reader, and to enable him
to realize the ideas which were familiar to the
circle in which she lived, at the moment when the
great drama was about to begin.

There is a great distance between the writer's
political conclusions and her starting-point. That
which took place in the mind of Madame J——
took place also in the mind of the nation. The
irresistible logic of facts brought her over, in the
first place, to the Republic; and then her patriotism
impelled her into the ranks of the Jacobin party.
The events which she relates day by day, and on
which she comments, explain the progress of her
ideas. She went straight forward to the point that
appeared to her to be that of safety. She was an
eye-witness of the perils which the common weal
incurred from invasion on the one hand, and
monarchical conspiracies on the other; and she
declared herself on the side of the only men who
were strong and bold enough to protect the demo-
cracy against enemies from within, and France
against the foreigner.

It is because Madame J—— belonged to a party
which has since been systematically calumniated,
that I have thought it right to publish her correspondence. A book, however humble it may be,

belongs to history, when it enables us to know what were the opinions, the habits, the ideas, or even the fears of a group of men whose influence upon the fate of our country was, at a certain moment, preponderating. And it seemed to me, also, that at the present time it might be useful to present to the public a picture of this Jacobin family, so truly worthy, so ardently French, grouped around a woman of superior mind, who in all the world loved only her husband, her two children, and—more dearly still—France.

EDOUARD LOCKROY.

TABLE OF CONTENTS.

1792.

Contents.

Contents.

THE GREAT FRENCH
REVOLUTION.

I.

ROMANS, *September* 20, 1785.

A THOUSAND thanks, my dear Jules, for your charming letter, and all the details of your journey.[1]
I needed that to enable me to sleep soundly. Only
fancy, my dear boy, I was driven from my retirement by my anxiety; I came into town yesterday
that I might be nearer at hand and so receive your
letter sooner. And to-day I have that dear letter
in my possession. And I have already read and
re-read the precious assurances of your affection.
I write to you from my new little cabinet. My
room is quite in order. Our good Thérése sits
there at her work in silence, and your little
Auguste,[2] who has grown good at last, plays about
and does not make much noise. Your aunts and
your uncle assembled here at post time, and I commu-

---

[1] Her son, then ten years and six months old, had just gone
to Paris with his father, there to enter on his studies.

[2] Her second son.

B

nicated the contents of your letter to them with tears
of joy and emotion. I sent immediately to the
house of our friends, the Miques, to inform them of
your safe arrival, and also that of your letter, for I
have not yet seen any one. My love of retirement
is increased by my sadness, and I would rather
be at leisure to think of you than given up to the
toil of society. I do intend, however, to go and
see Madame N—— one of these days. She passed a
long day with me at Les Délices, and she told me
repeatedly how much she loved my dear Jules. My
boy, your aunts, your uncle, your brother, our
maids, our man-servant, our work-people, all call you
" *Good Jules.*" That is a name, my son, which you
must always deserve. It is the best and the most
distinguished of titles. Be " good," my child, win
all hearts ; those of your superiors by obedience, those
of your companions by good-nature, and above
all, attach yourself to your dear uncle. Remember
what I said to you the night before we parted.

You have particularly requested me to give you
details, and that is just the difficult part of my
letter, for since your departure nothing has any
interest for me. I come and go, but I am absent-
minded and weary. I no longer study, and I cannot
read with any method. I write out your brother's
journal exactly, and I make him read all your com-
positions of 1784. But we have no more 'Berquin,'
our only reading is among our family reminiscences,
and these amuse him greatly. He read your letter

to-day, and was delighted to see his own name in it.
Never forget him, Jules! When you do not write
his name in full he frets. We often talk of you.
Yesterday we talked of no other subject all the way
from our own abode to the park. This morning we
went out walking again. I have no other particulars
to tell you. We walk and we talk of you—we talk of
you and we walk; in these two occupations we find
our most agreeable pastime. The rest is not worth
taking into account.

I beg of you, my dear Jules, to write your letters
in such a manner that your papa will not be able
to get a word into them. When he finds himself
obliged to take a fresh sheet of paper he will fill it,
I am sure; and do you, my dear, fill yours completely. All the new objects which meet your eyes
ought to furnish materials for your pen. Tell me a
great deal about your young friends. Paint their
portraits for me, describe their characters, their
minds, tell me about your games, and your conversations, and very soon about your occupations.
Above all things make yourself beloved; that
means, be good and amiable!

II.

AT LES DÉLICES,[3]
Thursday, September 29, 1785.

So then, the new objects with which my son is
surrounded do not efface me from his memory; and

---

[3] A country house in the village of Pisançon.

the attractions of his new position do not lead him to forget our simple country pleasures. I recognize you, my dear Jules, in all these indications of a good heart, and the loving regret which you express to me redoubles my own. I can no longer take pleasure in those fields where we were so happy together. I walk about them with a sad countenance and a bowed head; the sun shines out in all its strength in vain for me. My imagination surrounds it with clouds which it cannot pierce, and I know, only because I hear every one say so, that the weather is as fine as it can possibly be.

My good Jules, there is only one thing that can console me for all this pain; it is your application to your studies. Work hard, my child; remember the loving counsels of your mother, and above all, practise those virtues with which we have always endeavoured to inspire you. Make everybody love you; nothing is more sweet than being loved. Think also, my good Jules, of all you owe to the Supreme Being, for having given you existence, for having given you good parents, for having already bestowed innumerable favours upon you. Pray, and love God with all the strength of your young heart. Be pious and attentive in all your devotional exercises. Every day I implore of heaven that my son may be made a good man. Make my prayers heard by adding your own to them. Be good and virtuous. That you may be so is the one wish of my heart. I ask no other grace than this for my Jules, and I am sure that he already knows its value.

And so your papa is going to remain near your school. What a sacrifice he makes for you, my dear Jules, and how doubly dear to you that good father ought to become when you think of the proofs of affection he gives you. You are beginning your school-life under happy auspices indeed! Make up your mind that you will not be the last in the race, and think of the joy with which your fond mother will greet your success. I have so many things to tell you, to satisfy your curiosity, that I must pass on to details. We have finished our harvesting, and we have only twenty bins of grapes. Storms are so frequent and so terrible in this district that we are not the only sufferers. On Sunday there was a severe hailstorm in the canton of Genissieux, and the grape and corn crops were cut to pieces. Your poor cousin François is a heavy loser. His vineyard, which was ready for harvesting, was harvested by the hail.

Mademoiselle Reine Servan, Mademoiselle Félicité de M——, your two aunts, and the Chevalier, came early on Tuesday morning to pass the day. They arrived at nine, in the carriage belonging to Les Délices. After a slight supplement to their first breakfast we set off to the Château de Tendillon. We examined maps, we talked, we came back to Les Délices, where dinner was served. Manon surpassed herself. We had two excellent courses, pastry,

cream, truffled bread, a roast, entrées—nothing
was wanting; and at dessert we drank a bottle
of Lunel, which had such an effect on our
pretty young ladies that they sang and danced
merrily. After a game of loto came an excursion
to the vineyards, which I had arranged for that day,
and they filled a bin, then we had another pleasure:
we went down along the beautiful streamlets of
the Riousset to our meadows, and there the merry
party danced a " branle." Afterwards we found
seats at the end of the park, and Mademoiselle
Félicité, who has a fine voice, sang with your aunt.
The echoes, accustomed to repeat only plaintive
sounds, were quite joyful; they sent us back the
song and laughter of the happy party right willingly.
Then there was a great running of races from the
top of the meadow to the banks of the Isère. I
sighed to think that my dear Jules was not sharing
in festivities so suitable to his age, and I occasionally
wandered away from the merrymakers, in a medita-
tive mood, and thinking of my best-beloved. Your
brother read your letter for the young ladies very
well indeed. Mademoiselle Flavie, the eldest of
the P—— girls, gave him a bonbon-box, with a
picture of a little child on it, and the device, " I will
always love you." He did not want to have either
the box or the bonbons, because he was told that if
he accepted them he should thereby engage himself
to be Flavie's little husband. Every time marriage
was mentioned he gave back the box. This made

us all laugh, and he has kept the box, but it has not made him forget your letter, and the picture you sent him, which he prefers to all besides. When we came in at six o'clock in the evening, we found a charming collation prepared, and my young visitors, who had had plenty of exercise, ate as if that had been the first meal of the day. After that, all was over, and there was a general leave-taking, the carriage was brought round, and Joseph took the happy party home.

I forgot to tell you that, to do honour to the bottle of Lunel, we drank the health of M——, of M. Servan,[4] and of M. Jules. Are you not very glad to see your little name associated with the names of these great men? I trust that it may one day be worthy of them.

Press on with great strides; work, study, force yourself on. Think how you will delight the heart of that excellent father, who leaves everything in order that he may not leave his son. Think of your mother's pleasure, and also let your dear little soul catch some fire from the fair flame of glory. I speak to you as if you were a man, but have you not always been accustomed to the language of reason? Your heart makes you understand everything. Were you not, when you were here, my friend, my little confidant, my man of business? Adieu,

---

[4] M. Servan, Advocate-General to the Parliament of Grenoble, a learned publicist, and distinguished writer. He was the brother of General Servan, who was War Minister in 1792.

my Jules, give a thousand kisses for me to my friend *par excellence.* You know who that is.

III.

Although I was not vexed by your silence, my dear Jules, because your papa had informed me of its cause, I am, nevertheless, delighted that you have broken it, and I beg that you will occasionally steal a little time from your occupations to rejoice the heart of your fond mother by such a mark of your affection.

I stand in real need of consolation and encouragement in my miserable condition, thus parted from my best-beloved. You could not believe how much I suffer, and time, far from healing the wound, makes it deeper and more painful. My dear, dear Jules, it is two months to-day since I held you in my arms, and your papa and I have been parted for just the same time. But I must repress these ideas, and keep my feelings within the bounds of moderation. Profit, my dear boy, by the opportunities of your new position, to acquire wisdom and knowledge, and my sacrifice will become less painful to me.

You tell me of your occupations, but you do not say whether they are agreeable to you, and whether you are happy in this new state of things? What

does your tutor think of you. Endeavour, my dear
child, to respond to his efforts, and above all, be
grateful to him for them. Win his heart by your
application, and the hearts of your companions by
kindness and good-nature. Let my Jules be recognized as the son of a worthy father and a gentle
and sensible mother.

My dear boy, with what a father has heaven
blessed you! Love him, and imitate him; thus
you will do and be all that your fond mother can
desire. Talk to me constantly, always, about your
papa. How is he? What does he do? What
does he say? Am I continually in your thoughts
as you are in mine? Am I the subject of your
conversation as you are of ours? How I love you!
That one feeling is so fervent and so strong in my
soul that it cannot but exhale from it every
moment.

We have been in the country since Thursday;
but the cold, the wind, and the fogs, keep us shut
up, just as they did in town, and our fields have
lost all their charms. We do not want you here to
run about, we are ensconced in the chimney-corner,
where we eat Belleville chestnuts, and never without
saying, "Where are our dear ones? Why are they
not eating these with us?" Sometimes Auguste
says this quite of his own accord. Then he indulges
the funniest fancies. He makes you return unexpectedly; he knows very well all that would
happen in that case. He describes all our joyful

emotions, all the kissing and welcoming, and has the endearments appropriate to the occasion on the tip of his tongue. In short, these pretty little scenes of sentiment which he acts go straight to my heart.

My heart is sick, and always sick, although my bodily health is tolerably good. For six days of the week I am uneasy about you, and on the seventh, post-day, I am in a fever of alarm until the letters are delivered.

My Jules, I beg you will watch your papa, so that he may not fail to write to me, and also that you will write to our dear Clarisse. She is most impatient to receive a letter from her nephew. Write also to Madame Nuquet, and I will forgive you for a little gap in our correspondence in favour of those two dear friends. And so you are learning Greek! Learn many things, apply yourself to them all. I send you a kiss for the Greek, and I say to you in Latin, *diligo meum filium*. As for me, I no longer learn anything, and I make as much progress in ignorance as you make in knowledge. I am not teaching your brother anything except that *two and two make four*, and that a weak child ought to obey a stronger being. He is gentle and submissive, though bright and gay, and I am satisfied with him. I write up his journal for him every day, and he reads a great deal. That is all. He sends you a thousand kisses. Here is one of his notions; he found out on which side Paris is, turned towards the north, and with his little hand sent you the thousand kisses, by way of the wind, which would carry them to the point most contrary to their destination—to Africa or the great ocean.

Adieu! Take care of your papa. He is my best-beloved. Make him eat, sleep, rest, amuse himself, be happy, and love me. Do you love him with all my fervour. Tell him that you love him thus, and prove it to him incessantly. Think of me. Remember Epaminondas and Coriolanus, who took a double pleasure in doing right, from the sense of the joy they gave their good mothers. How I shall delight in your success in your studies, and your advancement in wisdom! Be good and virtuous, my Jules; those were the last words which I uttered, two months ago, in that sad adieu, and in them are expressed the most earnest desires of my heart. Bear in mind now, in your young days, that the most brilliant success, the greatest gifts of the intellect, are not so precious as the obscure virtues and the hidden treasures of a pure soul. Be good and virtuous. Adieu, my darling, my dear son, my good Jules!

IV.

Romans, *September 6, 1789.*[5]

You have written me two charming letters, my dear

[5] Her son, then fourteen years and six months old, had remained in Paris, while she went to Romans.

child, and I thank you for all the pleasure you have given me. I have called on all our friends to show them. They love you dearly, and have charged me to tell you so.

The troubles in Paris, and the difficulty in which they place the National Assembly, have something very alarming about them; and yet I cherish the fairest hopes. Up to the present time, all that menaced us with the worst evils has produced us the greatest good, and I like to believe that the same result will take place on this occasion. Our courageous representatives, after having braved the thunderbolts of despotism, will not allow themselves to be intimidated by the clamour of an excited multitude, and should the mob attempt to resort to dangerous excesses, the hero who is at the head of the Parisian militia[*] may be trusted to repress them. Everything is now very quiet in our province, and in those through which I passed on my way hither; but many châteaux have been burned; and what is much more cruel, a great number of peasants have been massacred by the soldiers of the local militia, or immolated by the hand of the executioner. Those unfortunate creatures, deceived by false edicts which were sent to them, believed that in burning the château and the title-deeds of their territorial lords, they were obeying the commands of the king. If ever culprits were worthy of indulgence, these certainly deserved it; nevertheless, they have

[*] M. de La Fayette.

been treated with the utmost barbarity. All this is most deplorable; but then one knows mankind, their passions and their prejudices; one is not so much astonished as grieved.

V.

To her Husband.

PARIS,
Tuesday, June 1, 1790.

This may be said to be " a sword-stroke in the water," for I know neither where you are nor where my letter may catch you. Yet I must write, if only to unburden my heart of some of its troubles. I must say one word of love to you, so that I may breathe a little more freely, and not be completely suffocated for want of utterance. If by any chance you are at Pisançon this evening, receive there, with many a kiss, the assurance of my strong attachment, which is of old date now—of the love that had its beginning there, and will have its end nowhere. I send you a thousand caresses from myself and my children; and I entreat you to come back to us upon the wings of the wind. We are like a body without a soul when you are not with us. M. Boucly,[1] who entertains MM. Barnave, Monnier, and Charles Lamotte at dinner on Thursday (Corpus Christi), would give more than I can say to number you among his guests. He said everything that

[7] Professor at the Collège Montaigu at Paris.

was flattering on that subject to Jules; so that, if my letter reaches you in time, and your philosophy can bring itself to bend before your patriotism, you will not receive this hint with indifference; and if you have no business on hand, you may allow yourself the pleasure of joining the party. I believe the scholars of the Montaigu School are preparing civic crowns for the brave defenders of liberty.

Your letter to M. Servan has been printed without the name of the writer, and is making a great sensation. M. S—— and his wife have had a singular adventure. Having taken refuge at the house of M. de Montelegien at G——, the château was besieged by the peasants, who suspected it to be a stronghold of aristocracy. The baron demanded that our municipal authority should give orders to his soldiers. On the refusal of M. F——, the baron threatened to shoot him out; to which he bravely replied that he would let himself be cut to pieces rather than he would sign an order contrary to the decrees of the National Assembly and to sacred humanity; and that the right thing was for them to proceed to the château unarmed, and induce the peasants to listen to reason. As the other municipals had signed the order, the soldiers marched, but all passed off quietly. Not a drop of blood was shed; not even a gun was fired in the air. Every one got off with a fright only, and M. S—— and his wife were brought back safely and quietly to Romans. The gunner, V——, who would not fire upon the people, was dismissed, and has passed through Romans. His comrades escorted him hither in full dress, and with military music; the soldiery of the faubourg received him with the greatest honours. He walked through the town crowned with laurel, and a superb repast was served to him. The municipal officers—F—— at their head —brought fifty bottles of the finest wine to regale the soldiery, and drank with them. They touched glasses with the gunner and with all the brave fellows. In short, this patriotic *fête* was so touching and so beautiful that all the women wept for joy. The gunner was escorted by the soldiers to the first municipality, where similar honours awaited him ; and he will be thus attended and honoured all the way to his destination. Such is the great lesson taught to soldiers who refuse to shed the blood of their fellow-citizens.

On Friday, M. de Saint-Priest asked the National Assembly for a grant of 2,645,000 livres for the first month's armament of the fourteen ships.

On Saturday, M. Necker made his appearance in the Senate, and spoke for two hours, displaying the vast resources of the kingdom. He drew a superb picture of the state of the finances. The receipts and the expenditure of 1790 will not only be balanced, but will leave a surplus of 12,000,000 in the treasury. He concluded by lamentations over the troubles which disturb the realm, and he made it plain that a vigorous exercise of the executive power would put an end to the terrible agitation that prevails. Then there was read a proclamation, sweet as honey, and signed *Louis*, which desires, among other things, that the national cockade be worn and honoured throughout the whole extent of this vast kingdom. On Sunday morning, our good king, mounted on a fine horse, rode almost alone from the Tuileries to the Champ de Mars to hold a review of 4000 citizen-soldiers. He complimented M. de La Fayette. He had the most charming congratulations addressed in his name to the troops : he was gay, and as happy as a king. The people were delighted ; the shouts of *vive le Roi!* came from all hearts. If we glance at the history of England, if we sound the depths of the human mind, we shall find material for reflection in all this.

VI.

PARIS, 1790.

The address sent to the king by the Commandant-General of the Guard in Dauphiné, the ci-devant pseudo-Baron de Gillier, is crawling and insidious ; and for that reason it has been received with distinguished favour by the ministers, who have presented this servile homage to his Majesty as a genuine expression of loyal devotion on the part of the brave citizen-soldiers. Nevertheless it was the baron only, or his prompter, who fabricated this document, and when it was brought to light, its guile was so quickly detected by the clear-sighted that a patriotic storm, from which the baron could only shelter himself by an equivocation, was raised. He gave a favourable interpretation to everything in the address that was susceptible of one, and he induced certain public busybodies to defend the rest. Thus did our brave Janus of the double face flatter himself that he might play the part of a skilful courtier at the court, and that of a good patriot in his province.

Now that he has been congratulated by his Majesty and that the adored minister has added to that transcendent favour two lines from his adorable hand, Janus forgets his double face, and shows himself as he is. But true and good patriots at Romans say what rumour with its hundred mouths repeats everywhere ; that the favour with which this address has been received is the exact measure of its cowardice and hypocrisy, that it tends to confirm the king in a fatal error, and that it may be the cause of lamentable dissensions among good citizens.

Here is another incident: M. Monier, a man of letters, a journalist, an excellent writer, and of sound principles, was bold enough to attack the baron's masterpiece, and the latter has already set the press groaning with his complaints. He has doubtless forgotten that the brave and generous Parisians have pulled down those formidable towers of the Bastille, which have served as a tomb for many innocent and unhappy citizens, whose great crime was an irreverence of the same kind as that of which M. Monier has just been guilty.

The baron ought to know, however, that the grand distributor of *lettres de cachet* exists no longer, and that in his place we have an honest *Procureur-général de la Lanterne.*[8] And as the baron asserts that he is at least *impartial*, no doubt the *Procureur's* first number will tell all France that such is the case. This *Procureur-général de la Lanterne* has achieved a brilliant reputation. His name is Camille Desmoulins, the title of his journal is *La Révolution de France et de Brabant*, and his style is the epigrammatical. He scatters Attic salt about in handfuls, and there is freshness as well as originality in his character. He combines French gaiety with Roman resolution. The baron may count upon the fidelity, the force, and the keenness with which he will render the fine shades of that *impartiality*.

I nevertheless warn the intrepid Desmoulins to beware ; for although the ci-devant pseudo-Baron de Gillier has not deigned to make the slightest mention in his address to the king of the august National Assembly which receives daily homage from the whole French nation, he has just written

[8] In the English version of M. Jules Clarétie's " Life of Camille Desmoulins " (Smith, Elder, and Co.), an account of the bestowal of this sinister appellation upon Camille will be found.

to the President, denouncing the rash and insolent
Monier, who had not the civility to be the dupe
of the polite dexterity of the baron. He has also
had an 'instruction' on this important affair for-
warded to M. de La Fayette, so that he may avenge
himself for the veracity and penetration of our
patriot journalists; and he has registered all these
doughty deeds in the broadsheet of his district.
M. Brissot de Varville is requested to publish them
in his also, so that the baron may not be cheated of
any of his glory. My letter would not be worth
printing, but I beg you will write a short patriotic
article on the subject, to sustain and encourage the
good citizens of Romans.

VII.

Easter Day, 1790,[9] 8 o'clock, a.m.

A good day, and a good deed, my dear boy. I
know you do not like your letters to be left un-
answered, and you see how eager I am to spare you
that little annoyance.

I have derived great pleasure from observing-
yours, in your stay at that charming place. Make
Madame P—— understand how grateful to her
I am for all her care of Auguste, and her kindness
to you. I am delighted that you are with her, and
I have so exalted an opinion of her kind-hearted-

[9] Her son has gone to Courcelles, near Pontoise, to pass
the Easter holidays with some friends.

ness that I am sure she treats you like her own
children. This happy thought smooths my pillow,
and I sleep soundly, being well assured that you
are quite happy with her. Tell this dear lady, in
confidence, that I regard her as one of our true
friends, and that I am penitent indeed for having
refused to join her delightful party. I should now
be with you and with her, and that would be much
better than my solitude; but I had to make the
sacrifice just now. At any other time I should not
have attempted it, for I suffer from unbearable
ennui. However, one half of your absence is over;
three full days lie behind me, and time weighs so
heavily upon me that I wonder how I have ever
got through them. Three days more, and we shall
be together !

Do you know that I have a little scolding to send
you? you never say a word about your papa. I
like you to tell me about him so much that your
letter seems quite incomplete when there is no word
of him in it, when you do not even say, " Papa
sends his love," " he is here," " he does this," " he
does that ;" these little details have an infinite charm
when one is talking to one's friends. And then,
you ought to tell me about Mademoiselle Adelaide,
and Pauline, and all your games; but you always
break off abruptly,—and like all men, small and
great, you do not know how to say little nothings.

I am very glad that Auguste is well. I think I
have done rightly in leaving him with you. Manage

him well, endeavour to be his mentor, and to get him to obey you. I had it in my head that he would write me a loving little letter, but perhaps he has done so, and that I shall receive it to-day. I do not tell you, my dear Jules, to behave well in every respect, because I reckon on your good sense, and your good heart, which is the best guide, because it inspires affection, politeness, and true kindness. Adieu!

VIII.

M. J—— TO HIS SON.

May 9, 1791.

You have written me a charming letter, my dear boy, and your father feels bound to thank you for the pleasure it gives, and the honour it does him. I have read it to all my friends, and there is not one of them who has not congratulated me with emotion upon my happiness in possessing such a son as you are. My dear, good Jules, while so many degenerate children extract food for their vanity from the merits of their ancestors, I, a father, of no utility to the world, as I well know, cannot but pride myself upon the merits of my son. It is not only of your style that I am thinking, although it is in general pure, noble, and lofty, like your mind; it is of your sentiments; it is of your patriotic ardour, and above all of the warmth with which you throw yourself into your friendships, and into the defence of all that is just and right. I congratulate myself on the attachment of M. Euvy [1] for you, but I congratulate him on the regard with which he has inspired you. I have not the slightest apprehension concerning the consequences of his arrest, or the movements to which that instance of persecution, and so many others, have given an impulse.

You and your mother will not fail to remember that you have heard me say repeatedly that La Fayette's hatred of the Jacobins, and their hatred of him, must sooner or later produce some terrible explosion. I am therefore not astonished that the moment is come, but I am astonished that it has been so long delayed. The crisis into which the dissensions of the Parisian army have thrown the capital is probably far from its termination; and so long as the staff of our sixteen battalions remains unchanged by the free election of the commune, you may expect to hear of fresh misfortunes every day. In reading your letter to our friends, I took care to moderate the alarm to which it gave rise. "Do not be uneasy," said I; "it is not true, however appearances may bear out the statement, that the majority of the Parisian soldiers have voted this impious oath, at which every friend of liberty must shudder. La Fayette himself took no share in it." . . . I do not doubt that those who opposed it were conquered, but I fear that they will make their conquerors pay dearly for victory, and that the streets

[1] A tutor, and also the editor of a political evening journal.

of Paris will run with blood before long . . . *Qucd omen Deus avertat!* . . . Another dread, more terrible still, and which has possessed me since the first dawn of the Revolution, is that the kings who surround France may form a league to stifle our newborn liberty, and thus prevent the contagion of what they call the *French disease.* They will not succeed, of that I am confident, but they may inflict much harm upon us. Adieu, my dear and dearest boy!

I lay myself at the feet of your excellent mother, and I adore her. Oh, my children, unite your homage with mine, and let us thank Heaven; you, for the most loving of mothers, I, for the most virtuous, the most sensible, and the most amiable of wives!

IX.

Paris,
Tuesday, August 2, 1791.

I have pitied you for your stay among that hateful lot of aristocrats; but the chapter of contrarieties is the longest and the most frequently repeated in the history of human life; it has a hundred thousand pages, and we must only put up with it, try to get used to it, and take up the shield of patience, never to lay it aside. I know people who have no notion of using that buckler, except against giants, and who let themselves be conquered by pigmies; that is to say, although they have strength to bear great contrarieties, they are weak enough to fume with impatience when they meet with small annoyances. I recommend the solution of this problem to your observant philosophy; as for me, I am at a loss to conceive how a man who would not be turned from his way by a rock in the path can stumble over a straw. Let us leave that point, and go on. How are you? How do you like the place where you are? How delighted I should have been to witness your meeting with the most loving of fathers, and to have thrown my arms around both of you. What do you think of your uncles, aunts, cousins, friends, and all the novelties that surround you?

I am as solitary as the sparrow upon the house-top, and it seems to me that I am alone in all Nature. Nevertheless here I am at Pontoise. And you are quite right, my dear boy, it is another world. What calm! What perfect tranquillity! I am already as much behindhand with the news of the day, as if I were in the depths of our woods at Romans, and as I have no other wish just now than to vegetate while I am frightened by the storm, I refrain from reading, talking, and I may almost say, thinking. The result is I have gathered from the conversations on all sides that the public mind is reliant, and the general belief is that we are nearing the port. As for the coalition of the Powers—*parturient montes, nascetur ridiculus mus.* This way of thinking leads to general repose.

The event (which is near) will prove which of the two classes, the *clear-sighted* or the *trusting*, has hit the mark. I, who believe blindly in the Providence of the Revolution, await with the firmest and most unhesitating faith a new and final miracle which will achieve our salvation. My dear, the wolves have always eaten the sheep, shall the sheep now eat the wolves ? That would be a little reversal of Nature, such as occurs only in terrible crises. Again I say, a miracle is wanted.

I don't want to talk politics, but before I quit the subject, tell me what the friends of the constitution at Romans have done. The banner of the Feuillants will have a great number of followers, if an end be not promptly put to this political schism. I would give anything to hear the oracles of my Apollo[2] upon all this : tell me what they are, and transmit every little word he says. I have had no news of him since you went away, and I reckon upon you to rekindle his tenderness for me. I wish I could be with you and him. I lend an ear, I fix my eyes, my heart beats, I listen to you, and I look at you from hence. Indeed, I am more with you than with myself, and I enfold you in my arms, making a chain of my love which ought to draw you closer.

Prince de Condé goes to Sweden, accompanied by the Bouillés, father and son, with leading military rank. The prince has made a statement by which he justifies himself, and accuses the nation. He

Her husband.

treats the National Assembly respectfully in it, however. If the document tells the truth, he pledges
himself not to draw the sword against us; and he
declares that all the Condés, past and present,
have been ardent partisans of liberty. If all these
people let a month pass without attacking us, and
that seems probable, we shall have no war before the
spring! Tell me exactly what your papa says, and
talk to me constantly of him and of yourself.

X.

Thursday, August 11, 1791.

As you say so truly, there does not exist in the
whole of Nature so true a joy as that of loving and
being loved. And yet, my dear son, that matchless
delight is so dangerous, that I advise you to endeavour to oppose the barrier of your reason to the
flood of your sensibility, for I dread the latter.

You have narrated the story of the death of our
dear Clarisse with so much feeling that I have wept
unrestrainedly over your letter. My dear Jules,
your sensibility is profound; endeavour to unite
with that quality, strength, which is the first of
virtues.

And now to the order of the day. I wrote to
your papa yesterday, and told him of all my doings;
I also imparted to him my observations upon the
state of public feeling, which, in the canton I am
leaving, is that of mild and wise moderation. The

people admire the National Assembly, and adore the constitution. They regard the ship as already in harbour; they have little fear of enemies from the outside, and they ridicule those that are within; in short, a calm prevails, with nothing to trouble it but the scarcity of money that is felt everywhere; but they say, "We shall not be caught by this means, any more than by the famine which they contrived to drive us into submission." Our constancy and our courage will conquer everything. The love of the constitution inspires all hearts with a certain amount of heroism. On that point public opinion is formed and mature; and respect for the law is assuming such power, that, just or unjust, the people desire to obey it. On all sides one hears those words, "*The law, the law.*" If the law could be had without magistrates, as my friend Jean Jacques wants to have medicines without doctors, we should behold the reign of Astræa, but men spoil everything by their want of tact. *Everything is good as it comes from the hands of Nature,* but all grows corrupt in those of man. The law is good in principle, but the administration is often evil.

My dear, a great contempt for wealth, and, as the Gospel says, not to have two weights and two measures, that is what would give real credit to our Themis, and make every knee bend to her. I hope the new *régime* will bring forth virtue, and therefore it is that I worship the Revolution. You know that

I am not one of those who have lost but little through its action; my health and my tranquillity, without reckoning my happiness, destroyed by the perpetual absence of your father, all suffer by the the Revolution.

I have been obliged to relinquish a great deal of reading which led me into dejection. It is in the nature of lofty souls only to love certain things that are too high for others. It is best to descend to the ordinary level and to think that " the better is the enemy of the good." I have therefore cured myself of my Roman fever, which, however, never made me give into Republicanism from the fear of civil war. I shut myself up, with the animals of every kind, in the sacred ark of the constitution, and I wait with impatience until the dove be sent out to bring us back the olive branch.

See how all our legislators are striving to merit our respect! It is a remarkable circumstance that the hall of the Assembly resounded with the applause of the galleries, when the decree that fettered our electors was revoked, and from the eighty-three corners of France arises the cry, " A new legislature! " This has the double advantage of urging that which exists to raise itself to the pitch of elevation to which public opinion often lifts it, as if in spite of itself, and also of encouraging that which is to come to display the greatness that we expect from it. Tell me, dear child, what is the general disposition of B——, and whether the

Jacobins have turned into Feuillants. How many things I long to know!

I dined at Madame Soret's, at Pontoise, with two aspirant deputies. One had been dining recently with Barnave, whom he knows. He assured me that he found him singularly changed for the better, · and that his system of politics is now that which all sound thinkers approve. *Ecce homo!*

I must tell you that the country-people see the Revolution just as the occupiers of front boxes at the opera see the play. The illusion is perfect. We Parisians are placed so as to get a view of behind the scenes! We see the actors changing their dresses and their rôles; we see the ropes by which the gods are hauled up into Olympus, and the machine off which the Savoyard boy winds the rolls of silver paper that pass for running water, &c.

I should not be at all surprised if I should soon have to tell you that our king is going away, has gone away, &c., &c., and " the guard who watches at the gate of the Louvre" will know nothing about it!

I was assured to-day that Santerre had been obliged to fly. The members of the club of the Cordeliers are being prosecuted. The white flag has replaced the red since last Sunday.

XI.

To her Husband.

Sunday, August 14, 1791.

It seems to me, my dearest, that I am more yours when here than when I am in other people's houses, and that strong reason, added to all those which make me passionately fond of my *chez moi,* renders it so dear to me at this moment that I am almost as much pleased as if I had found you here. Your spirit is always with me, and as one is more familiar with spirits than with men, I say to it constantly, "you foresaw this—you told me six months ago what is happening now." Seriously, though, you possess a Socratic genius which unveils the future to your vision, and I would give much to be able to consult you upon what may happen to us a month hence. Since you look with the eyes of a lynx into the book of destiny, and that your penetrating glance takes in both sides of the leaf at once, tell me, my dear "genius," what is it that fate has in store for us? As for me, I tender you a fresh tribute of praise, since I have trodden other regions. I have seen patriots who love the Revolution, but who, being superficial, remain on the surface, and are content with everything. They believe the fables of Métis implicitly. I have maintained a most strict silence on many points; few love things after our manner—or have the holy love of humanity and the still more holy love of virtue that inflame our hearts; and those two loves are unknown to many people who make a great noise in the world. Ambition, interest, all the petty human passions exercise their sway over those who think; and those who have not the honour to think at all, are so numerous and such sheep-like creatures that they only need a Guillot for a shepherd to lead them all to the shambles.

As I desire to die peacefully when my time comes, and not prematurely as a martyr to my feelings, I have given up all association with persons who show me too plainly the chains with which we are being bound. I cannot break a link of the fetters, and all those which have spikes on them wound me. I hardly ever read now; I give way to a kind of paralysis, or rather, I bestir myself to my true and natural avocations—the education of Auguste, and my spinning-wheel. The upshot of my observations is this : when one is Spartan, or Roman, at Paris, one is also somewhat Huron.[3] That will come; certain metamorphoses take more than a day. But there really does exist strong public spirit, and a genuine love of the constitution. In short, there is a great deal of confidence, perhaps too much; but *let us await the end : from afar on the horizon comes with fury the most terrible of the children, &c.*

[3] The reader will find frequent familiar references to the writings of Voltaire in the letters of Madame J——. They were so thoroughly understood by her husband and son that they are not formally indicated.

The application of the fable is that the oak is uprooted, while the reed bends to the storm unharmed; the reed is our constitution, it bends, but will not be broken; I know that it will resist the winds, and hold out against the fury of the tempest. Robespierre, Pétion, and Buzot, our good and priceless triumvirs, if all the good that you proclaimed has not been done, how much evil have you not prevented! I would that the eighty-three departments were thoroughly convinced of their obligations to those who have been so unjustly designated, even in the capital, by the odious name of factious persons. But for them, and the courage of the brave Parisians, wise and foolish, you would have reaped no fruit from all the labours and cares of your Assembly, except chains and insult.

You are about to nominate new legislators; on them rest the hopes of the country. Each one thinks that there will come from the wilds of the provinces Cato, Cincinnatus, Aristides, Fabricius, multiplied by scores. Above all, no priests, and no *beaux esprits;* but worthy people, who do not care for money! Make a good choice, my dear. There is something I want to whisper in your ear; I do not think you have the right to be an elector or a deputy, because of the decree which requires domicile. I have on that head (I mean the deputation) principles which are all the firmer because they are founded on the purest virtue; but I will enter into no explanation on the subject until we meet. I defy your philosophy to place me in the wrong, and the tenderest friendship, as well as the most exacting love, to find aught in my heart to reprove. I wish it could be laid bare before you; I would glory in the inspection.

The Dauphin is no longer to bear that title; he is to be called simply by his name. M. Camus has had inserted amongst the constitutional decrees, one enacting that henceforth the nation shall not pay the debts of the king or the royal family.

The representatives at the National Assembly, elected by each departmental assembly, are to be chosen from the eligible citizens of the department only. The inscribed electors of each department are to meet to elect so many representatives as their department is to return, and supplementary representatives in the proportion of one-third of the former. The members of the legislative body are eligible for the succeeding election, but not afterwards until after an interval of two years. The representatives elected in the departments are not to be representatives of any one department, but of the whole nation.

No mandate can be imposed on them either by the primary assemblies or by the electors. I do not know why I pass my time in copying for you things that you doubtless know better than myself I prefer telling you that what pleased me most in Jules' letter was its not containing one word about politics; for that proves the absolute calm of your part of the country. The letter was sent after me to Pontoise, but I received it to-day. I am pleased to see by it that you are well and strong : which means that you are happy and tranquil *in petto*.

Although I regret your absence, I am glad to think you are not in this Babel of Paris, and I am already beginning to be uneasy at the prospect of the winter. I hope my sister will come and help me to bear that cross. What makes it so heavy, is seeing the animosity that is fostered between the citizen and the soldier. This accursed *esprit de corps* warps and destroys every generous feeling. For my part I should be glad if all the blue coats in the world were made into a bonfire, and nothing would please me more than to see our National Militia dressed in all the colours of the rainbow, like the troops of Henry IV.

" Vanity of vanities : all is vanity ! "

This reminds me that Danton, Santerre, Desmoulins, &c., are remanded for further examination, and others are ordered to be arrested. The " Friend of the People " and the " Orator " fulminate every day as usual. I read Andoin's and Pestel's papers, the *Journal de Paris* and the *Moniteur*.

XII.

Saturday, August 20, 1791.

To-day I am going to talk politics and philosophy with Mr. Secretary.[5] You must, my dear child,

___

[5] Her son was then sixteen years and five months old. He

employ all the wisdom and prudence of an experienced man in the duties you are called upon to fulfil. Remember that among the twenty-five millions who people this great realm of France, there is hardly one in a hundred who has raised himself to the height of the Revolution, or who understands all that your fresh and energetic mind feels and conceives so easily, like those valiant Romans with whom your recent studies have made you intimate. If you have observed judiciously, you will have become impressed with the real public spirit which in general is indulgent and moderate, though firmer than one could naturally expect from French imaginations. As for me, I have found that even the most ordinary minds have advanced a century in the last two years, and I have been careful myself to follow the plan you so cleverly suggested to me. I have bent, that 1 might rise up more erect than before.

Let us remember what Lafontaine says: "Plus fait douceur que violence." In every part of France they are delighted with the constitution ; it is the rallying-point. Some think our legislators might have done better, some maintain that they have done their best—interminable quarrels result from this difference of opinion ; but if we consider the general corruption of men degraded by more

had just been appointed secretary to a patriotic society at Romans, whither he had gone to pass his holidays with his father.

than twelve centuries of slavery, we may think ourselves lucky to obtain half-benefits, and live in hope that with time a complete regeneration will be effected in spite of every obstacle. If our second legislature is a worthy one, as we hope it is, what good it will do even though we have so few good laws! It will be supported by public opinion, which, in general, is as pure as the air of our fields. Without resorting to innovations what miracles may be worked! In short, dear child, the sense of responsibility, once roused to vigorous action, might give an impetus that would raise us at once twenty degrees. Paris is as still as a pond, except for certain private feuds which daily give rise to tragic scenes.

Thursday, 25.

The constitution is to be presented this week. All sorts of theories and guesses about it are afloat. Nostradamus himself was not more extravagantly incoherent. The king of the constitution seems to me so well treated—all the gems of the crown have been picked up and replaced so carefully by our legislators—that the bouquet they are about to present to his Majesty on Thursday will I think be grateful to the most courtly nostrils. They smell the sweet savour of the Civil List, which is maintained in its integrity. Some think the blindness of the opposition party will engage the king in a resistance which may have incalculable results. Nothing can approach the insolent security of our enemies: as for me I take refuge in the miracles that I expect from the Providence of the Revolution which has already accomplished so many. I hope it has one all ready prepared for the order of the day on Thursday. I am not much afraid of the Foreign Powers who are put forward as a scarecrow. My theory is based on the affairs they have in hand, on the alarm they must feel at the Rights of Man that are circulating everywhere, and on the prevarication and crooked policy of all the ministers. There are divisions on all sides, and the winter will be our security, from now until such time as they are agreed on the important question of the attack. As for our (black) army and our princes who are its chiefs; had the wind of the wrath of the National Assembly blown patriotically upon them, they would have been annihilated. This Assembly might bear us to the summit of honour and prosperity. Oh, accursed corruption! They say that our Jacobins are coming back to favour, and that the star of the Feuillants is on the wane. I approve of the policy of certain societies which have kept up a double correspondence, so that they might judge with more certainty where the real patriotism lay. As for the others I am sure of nothing; I see but few people, and I have quarrelled purposely with the hot-headed journalists, because they were too much in the right not to be also very much in the wrong, and they annoyed me personally

without any advantage to public affairs, in which
I can do nothing.   Doubtless you remember the
feverish agitation they used to cause me, and which
used to deprive me of appetite and sleep.

I shall not go to G—— as I told your papa.   I
do not feel in the humour to pay too dear for that
pleasure.   Auguste torments me to go and enjoy the
country air.   The monotony of my retirement preys
upon his mind.   I am delighted that you are enjoying yourself : to know that you are well and happy,
enables me to endure all my privations with courage.
Remember the adage, *Mens sana in corpore sano,*
and do your best to preserve the treasure of health.
Your papa seems to enjoy the *far niente* at Romans
as much as at Paris, and I am almost afraid that he
is losing there the energy which used sometimes to
animate him here, and made him talk so as to carry
us away in a sort of rapture.

His philosophy penetrates too far into the human
heart to permit him to expect from it all he could
wish, so his strong mind seeks to benumb itself.
But I adore him, my child, for a thousand reasons,
the first of which renders the enumeration of all the
others needless ; he is a sincere friend of virtue, and
if, in your life, you meet many like him, thank
heaven for it. Such men are the honour and happiness of humanity.   Is he still your president, and
have your electoral meetings begun ?

I have just been reading the newspaper.   Complaints have been made to the Assembly about

certain societies of friends of the constitution here
and there. The society of Marseilles, and several
of the societies of Normandy, have been especially
attacked. The Abbé Fauchet, Bishop of Calvados,
has, it is said, excited these societies by preaching
maxims contrary to the new doctrine, persuading
them to throw down the statues of the kings, &c.,
&c. One municipality has brought a criminal action
against him, and now M. Vreillard has procured a
decree for his arrest and prosecution. Pétion
objected, but he has been overruled. Reflect upon
this, and put yourself under the protection of
Minerva's shield, for our interest and your pre-
servation.

I send you by Gaspard, who started on Saturday
by the diligence, the key of the little cupboard at
Les Délices. All the records of your childhood are
locked up in it. Respect those memorials of our
vigilance and love for you.

Yesterday there was a splendid *fête* in the
Champs Elysées : all Paris was there. Lots were
drawn for a lamb, just as at the butchers' *fête* we
saw at Lyons. Do not suppose we are dull, the
capital was never more brilliant, more noisy, more
magnificent, more opulent. Never at any moment
was there more dancing or more dissipation of all
sorts, and that in the midst of the direst poverty, and
the most terrible scarcity of money. Our natural
French gaiety remains with us, and tempers all our
misfortunes.

XIII.

From M. J.

Paris, *August* 30, 1791.

Only one of the three plans you have proposed to me seems advisable for the moment; and I am sorry to say it is not that which you appear to wish me to adopt. To speak plainly, my dear child, your idea of going away alone into the country to complete your studies, would strike me as extremely foolish and ridiculous if I did not take into consideration your youth and inexperience. Setting aside the *ennui* which profound solitude would soon produce, do you think you know enough to be able to learn, without help, all that still remains for you to acquire? Doubtless, as you justly observe, your real studies are now about to begin, and that is precisely why you are more in need of masters and guides than ever you were; that is why a residence in Paris is the only one that will suit you, the only one in which your education can be completed with success. If you were left to your own resources in some retired place, you would soon feel your weakness, and would regret the help of every sort from which you had voluntarily separated yourself. To understand an author properly, it is frequently necessary to have recourse to twenty other works which can only be found in large libraries; and very often, books do not suffice to explain books. Intercourse

with the dead is of no great use, unless it be combined with acquaintance with the living. Besides, my
dear child, if you wish to turn your studies to the
advantage of your fellow-creatures, the human heart
should be, above all, the subject of your meditations ;
and do you think you will learn to know men by
eschewing their society? Would you not, on the
contrary, run the risk of forming false ideas of them,
and of constructing a chimerical theory that would
be with difficulty dispelled by subsequent experience? If you had made your preparatory studies
in the country you would have been obliged to come
to Paris to finish them ; and yet you talk of leaving
this abode of all the talents to go and cultivate your
own amongst our farm-labourers—simple and excellent folk, I grant you, but coarse and ignorant. You
talk of seeking light in darkness, like as your mamma
says, an astronomer who should go down into the
cellar to observe the courses of the stars. But I
have said enough, more than enough, to convince
you of your error. Your course of studies in
the schools is not yet finished, as you say, and I
think you might, with advantage, go through the
customary two years of philosophy. If you prefer
studying logic and ethics at home, and joining
private classes for chemistry and mathematics, I
have no objection. This year will be a very good
one. I hope the aristocracy may burst with rage
when they find we are not starving. We shall soon
be busy with the elections ; I think the primary

assemblies will be convened for the 23rd of this
month.   I hardly dare tell you how much every one
here seems to regret that I cannot be nominated,
nor how pleased I am at not being obliged to risk
an election.   You must not be vexed with me, dear
Jules, nor accuse me of being a bad citizen.   I may
venture to say that no one is more truly patriotic
than myself; but, at the same time, nobody knows
his own capacities better; and I feel that the
narrowness of my intellect, joined to its indomitable
idleness, would render me absolutely incapable of
filling any public function.   You must also think
thus of your father, without loving or esteeming
him any the less for it; for ignorance is not a vice,
and idleness in a man who is nothing, is 'at the worst
only a defect.

XIV.

Sunday, September 4, 1791.

I have had no sign of life from father or son
since the 20th and 24th of August.   I know, by
means little short of a miracle, that the father's
election was contested in order that it might be
all the more gloriously confirmed.   And I learn
from Seigneur, a shorthand reporter ot the Jacobins, who passed two hours with me to-day, that a
certain address at Romans signed M. A. J. was
read, and rapturously applauded at the meeting,
and that there were loud cries of "Print it!"
Just imagine how pleasant it is when news of

that sort, relating to one's dearest friends, is brought
to one's ears by mere rumour. I can assure you,
gentlemen, that I am often asked whether I am a
relation of yours, or merely have the honour of
bearing the same name. Young Seigneur gave me
a sketch of the Jacobins that would not have disgraced Tacitus. Every one worth electing was
returned in triumph—thirty-seven deputies all at
once—the Assembly is flourishing, and the Feuillants are nowhere—that needed only a good blast of
wind. Camille Desmoulins is there—I mean at the
Jacobins' club—as if nothing had happened; our
Bishop of Calvados has succeeded in obtaining a
triumphant justification : he is elected deputy. In
short, my ideas are quite confused, so great is my
joy to find black calumny missing every mark. Our
elections in Paris surpass our hopes, Garan de
Coulon, Lacépède, and Brissot, make us hope for
others who are called for by patriotism but held
back by the coalition. At Versailles, Lecointre and
Soret, and, observe the vicissitudes of all things
human ! Cardinal Loménie, Brienne the minister,
representatives of the French people—the one a fugi-
tive and outlawed, the other oppressor oppressed.

You may imagine my anxiety, Jules, about all that
has happened, and all that is happening at Valence.
My very heart and soul are there. I hardly breathe
for the terror that is ever before my eyes, and the
dangers I foresee; but the public hope imposes
silence on me, so I repress my own thoughts and

personal feelings. I am longing to know what has been drawn from the fatal urn, and I shall bring all my philosophical reflection to bear upon it; but uncertainty is the worst of evils, and indeed you ought to have made it a matter of conscience to abridge mine. According to the reckonings of my imagination, and the impatience of my heart, I ought to have heard from you two days ago : I am a prey to the most intense anxiety. You, Jules, who are naturally sensitive, would have spared me a great deal if you had given yourself the trouble of telling me what is passing around you. Neither aunt, nor brother, nor sister, nor relations, nor friends send me one word. I write in every direction, right and left. Is it the post that keeps back your answers? Good night, I am going to supper and then to bed —that is wiser than hanging one's self. . . .

It is Monday morning, six o'clock, and I am again with you, my dear child. The hope of receiving a letter to-day has awakened me to pleasant thoughts. Pandora's box stands on my table, like a snuff-box.

Take care, my dear son, to maintain all through life a certain punctuality in your correspondence; for, in the absence of those we love, a slip of paper will often contain health, happiness, and tranquility; and negligence in writing, or the foolish habit of turning a short letter into a laborious affair, often inflicts excessive pain on those who are waiting and expecting. It will be three weeks next Saturday since you last wrote to the tenderest of mothers ; the pious Æneas would have considered that a crime against Nature. I have often called you by the noble name of Æneas ; let your good heart glory in trying to deserve it.

Let us talk politics. Pastoret has taken Brissot's place in the third nomination of the deputies of the capital. The ballot, which supported them both, returned Pastoret at the last turn ; but, for to-day, it will be our dear Brissot, in spite of the cabal. M. Pastoret is a bit of a turncoat, I think.

The Tuileries were opened yesterday ; everybody was there, and the crowd was immense. The royal child was exhibited with great pomp, his mother and his aunt taking him in their arms by turns to present him to the people. The " executive power "[6] has formally announced his decision not to leave Paris. All the foolery has recommenced ; the mass yesterday at the château was magnificent, the music superb, and to loud cries of " *Long live the king* " I added " *the constitution.*" His acceptance is expected with the greatest calm and the most sanguine hopes. He would be very hard to please if he were not satisfied, but then Lafontaine says,—

> " C'était assez de biens ; mais quoi !
> Bien ne remplit les appétits d'un Roi ? "

We shall see. Lafayette is charged to form his military establishment himself : that is another touchstone by which to estimate how many carats there are in the gold. That is a commercial metaphor taken

[6] The king was so denominated by the revolutionary party.

from trade which you must get explained to you· if
you do not understand it, for I cannot tell you what
it means. Ask your father to criticize my writing ;
he alone holds the clue to the labyrinth of my
thoughts, and as I always write *currente calamo*, I do
not trouble myself about the lights and shades in
my ideas. Light and shade make the finest effects
in painting, and not always a bad one in my careless
feminine scribble.

Trv to accustom yourself, dear child, to my
style ; *car le vase est imbibé, l'étoffe à pris son pli.*
And there is Lafontaine again. I quote him on
every occasion, for his shafts hit all our weaknesses.

They are playing a new piece at the Français,
called *Virginie*, or *Les Decemvirs*. Its great success
lies in its allegorical lines :—

" Pour nous donner des lois il faut avoir des mœurs."

There are a thousand pointed allusions in it that
bring down the house. The piece will take, for the
Regina del Mondo has sworn it, and she is the queen
of monarchs. Adieu, my dear, my very dear child,
the hope of my heart is the sublime conviction
that you will always be a firm friend of Virtue; listen
to no teachings but hers, and look neither to the
right nor the left, but push on to the heights, even
though you tread on sharp blades to reach them.
Watch over your youth. Telemachus himself, without Mentor, would have seen his white hairs defiled
by the faults of his earlier years. Do you shelter

yourself always under Minerva's shield. I am very fond of that image, Jules.

Cerutti was elected deputy yesterday.

XV.

PARIS, *October* 9, 1791.

I write to you to-day, dear child, intoxicated with joy and pleasure. Your father is here. I cannot describe to you the touching scenes, the content of mind, the fulness of joy, the delightful feelings that swell my heart. In truth, no power of words could do that. Only a sensitive and loving nature like mine can understand these things. The amusing part of it all is, that when I saw your father at the street door, I ran to tell your brother, who was lying down resting in one of the furthest rooms of the apartment. He wanted to run, but his poor leg did not, so limping along we arrived at the door, which in our agitated eagerness we could not open. At last, however, we were locked in each others' arms, crying, laughing, ready to die of joy. Your poor brother was as delighted as I was. I fancy his illness has developed his intellectual faculties as well as his frame, and he has progressed more in his convalescence since yesterday than in a fortnight before. Happiness is a sovereign balm for all evils, and his father's presence was indispensable to his recovery. I fear I must own, my son, that my maternal tenderness is often prejudicial to you, and your father's sound sense, which he knows how to unite to the most indulgent affection, will correct to some extent the undoubted harm I have done your brother by taking care of his body at the expense of his mind. In times of trial the mind should be allowed to struggle with itself, so to speak, in order to acquire strength; whereas I have been enfeebling his by my anxious solicitude, and all those little attentions that weaken fortitude.

Once more I am under the shelter of your father's care. I feel my strength returning, and my mind becoming more vigorous; and our invalid, without being less cared for, will receive more manly treatment. I sadly needed your wise father in this difficult passage from convalescence to health; never was he given back to me more opportunely. I weary Heaven, my child, with my thanksgivings.

As for you, I have many things to tell you privately. My anxious eyes follow you, and I have discovered things in your own and your aunt's letters that fill my mind with misgivings. Be on your guard against your imagination and your sensitiveness as your greatest enemies; strive against your natural impetuosity; remember that you can only, as yet, lisp the language of reason, though you think yourself a full-fledged philosopher. My child, my child, instruct yourself; be on your guard against yourself; believe no false and deceitful praise. Happily you are virtuous by nature. With that one goes a long way if one measures one's steps.

XVI.

Paris, *October* 20, 1791.

I have seen no one since your father's return. The continual rains, and the distance we are from town, are insurmountable obstacles. The dear father goes every day to the National Assembly,[7] so that your brother and I are as lonely as sparrows, and that makes his convalescence a little dull. The remains of the wound in his leg and the bad weather combined, confine us completely to the house. My habit of *far niente* is strengthened, which is very excusable after such a terrible shock ; but it makes the hours still longer, so we impatiently await your return, because the presence of our friends Vierge and Jules will brighten up our quiet retreat. We shall have some one to talk to, and something to talk about—all that is necessary for happiness.

M. Soret,[8] that real friend, regrets sincerely that your father is not his colleague; all our friends are patriotically vexed about it, and regard the Dauphinois as idiots for having rejected a man of his stamp. Perhaps, dear Jules, it is a providential benefit—there are always two sides to a medal.

I had got so far with my letter when yours arrived.

Excellent, my son, excellent. So long as reason

[7] He was "deputy-supplementary." He only became deputy later on, at the Convention.

[8] Deputy for Pontoise at the Legislative Assembly.

E

holds the helm, the bark will not be shipwrecked. But please to reflect that from now till the time when you have to pay the debt which every individual owes to Society and Nature, you will have visited so many countries, and seen so many people, that you must not be in a hurry to make your choice. Have a wholesome dread of the changes so common at your age, and that you may not be inconstant beware of promising to be faithful. You are still young, my dear Jules.[9] Young man, young man, tremble lest you be the dupe of your own precocious wisdom! Be assured that to be able properly to recognize what is good for one's happiness, one must have learned more from experience than you have, and that ten additional years must pass over your young head before you can have attained the maturity necessary for many things. In the meantime remain, as you say yourself, master of your own heart, that is the noblest empire a man can have; and since you know how dangerous are the delusions of a too lively imagination and a too sensitive heart, and that you mistrust yourself, you possess the clue that will save you from being lost in the labyrinth of passion.

One thing that I hardly think it necessary to warn you against, is the being in too great haste to show your little productions. On that point you should exercise the greatest reserve and the most delicate tact. Nothing is more ridiculous than to

[9] Jules was then sixteen and a half.

talk about one's self. There is a lady of your own and my acquaintance who has that defect. She seems silly to me, although she has plenty of cleverness, for the one reason that she introduces the *ego* everywhere. Real modesty, or proper and decorous pride, can keep itself in the background without being a loser thereby. The former, and the best, by the action of its own lovely nature ; the latter from calculation. But this latter is good if the other be wanting, for it keeps us clear of the cunning snare set for us by our self-love, and preserves others against annoyance. But enough, my son, I always seem to be preaching ; it is not, however, in my maternal capacity, but because I have a natural inclination to reflection, and it is my way with my friends as well as with you. Talking of friends, I count on you to be my best and most precious friend after your father. The greatest confidence and the tenderest sincerity are the terms of that friendship. And indeed, my son, I expect nothing from you but joy, pleasure, and consolation. *Barnave is full of life and health, but dead to immortality.* That is my own opinion, good or bad, as you please to find it.

XVII.

PARIS, *October* 20, 1791.

You do not appeal to me in vain, my son. Your father, whose sole earthly desire is the happiness of his children, and whose enlightened philosophy is

E 2

above prejudice, leaves you free to choose the career
that suits you best. Good conduct in every condition, inflexible practice of the virtues of which he
sets you the example, is all he asks of you, and that
more for your own happiness than for his. As for
me, my son, I am not so easy to please, and I want
to have a little explanation with you. In the first
place, I am much hurt at the manner in which you
censure the education we have given you, and your
quotations of Jean-Jacques are as little applicable
to the subject as they can well be, for so we have
lived ourselves and brought you up. Walks in the
Palais-Royal are no more contagious for you than
for us. Those who have fixed ideas upon the
real value of things are not easily dazzled by
tinsel. Now, these ideas are either impressed in
ineffaceable characters upon you, or you will
never conceive them, but will find, even in the
remotest province, a stumbling-block for virtue
whose foundation is so weak that it requires prop-
ping up on every side.

My son, you are a man, and born to live amongst
men. At Paris, Peru, or Japan; in the provinces,
in the villages, vices and virtues are to be found.
It is necessary to know men and investigate their
characters, before deciding on the places where they
are better or worse, and that in which it suits you
best to settle. All things considered, the provinces
are perhaps more dangerous than the capital, and
the young man who wishes to isolate himself here

is a thousand times more free and more secure from
the dangers of passion, than within the limits of a
small town where he cannot get away from tempting
objects. There is a kind of corruption here; but so
vile, so abject, that I believe it to possess no danger
for any one with ever so little elevation of soul, and a
naturally honest heart. Examine yourself, seriously,
my son, and be sincere with yourself. Perhaps the
three months you have passed at Romans have been
more prejudicial to your moral being than the six
years which you passed in the capital, in studies
that you now regard, in your wisdom, as futile; and
with that same senseless wisdom you answer your
father with one of Rousseau's arguments: " Un
sage gouverneur doit commencer à soigner le
physique." Is that a reproach ? Is it a lesson ?
Poor boy ! Do you know that from the moment of
your birth every means has been employed to make
you healthy in body as well as in mind? Do you
know that we lived in the country during your childhood on purpose to strengthen your body? and
that we gave up all our own pleasures to come here
with you and clear a field of which you alone will
reap the harvest? Do you not know that where
other parents confide their children to strangers,
and let them take their chance in the pursuit of
knowledge, your father and mother have followed
you to keep you under the shadow of their wings ?
Have you not been happy within the shelter of your
home, engaged in the occupations suitable to your

age ? The tranquillity of our domestic pleasures, the companion we gave you to stimulate you in your work and share your enjoyments, have all these been unavailing to make you happy ? Your success and good conduct in your student career filled me with the pleasantest fancies; I firmly believed in your happiness until the moment when you told me you had not been happy.

I remember, now, one of your arguments— " Happiness is nothing but the absence of misfortune." You have enjoyed perfectly good health these last six years ; you have had all the good things of this life in abundance; you have accomplished your duties in a way which induced us to believe you took pleasure in them ; you have been tenderly cherished by your parents. No reproach, no complaint, no punishment has ever warped your mind. Your conduct in childhood, marked by the approbation of the best of fathers and the most indulgent of mothers, has won for you the friendship and esteem of all our friends. These, my son,—I appeal to your justice—these are the misfortunes you deplore. Be careful how you blaspheme Providence.

XVIII.

To her Husband.

Paris,
April 16 (fourth year of liberty), 1792.

I write to you, dear husband, in a sort of trans-

port of pleasure. The *fête* passed off amid all the
pomp, the magnificent simplicity, and the profound
tranquillity of a festival of the people. Nothing
could be more splendid. I saw it all with my own
eyes, and I had but one regret, not to have him by
my side who first taught me to feel and appreciate
real beauty. Why were you not there? Odious
journey! But peace, my heart; let us forget our
private grief in our great public joy, and return to
the account of the *fête*.

I was placed, under the auspices of our excellent
Mdlle. Canot, in the balcony of a handsome
apartment on the first floor, on the boulevard
opposite the Rue de Montmartre. The windows
were filled with spectators the whole length of the
boulevards. The crowds of people all along the
pathway was so great that we began to think the
procession would never pass, and it was the same
from the Barrière du Trône to the Champ de Mars.
Nothing could be more imposing than the calm and
serenity that reigned. The procession was delayed
at the last moment by some prudent and moderate
arrangements, which gave a different character to
the *fête*, without exactly changing the original programme; the soldiers of Château Vieux, who were
to have been on the car with the women and children and the emblems of plenty, all walked in a
group among the other citizens. The dense crowd
ranged itself in a line with marvellous order and
precision, and the police regulations were never

better nor more quietly observed. The *tables of the law*, carried by strong men, came immediately after the first groups, which were composed of people carrying banners in honour of liberty. Then came the portraits of great men, adorned with civic crowns. Stones from the Bastille, on which were engraved " Liberty," " Equality," were carried on a car ornamented with the tri-colour. After that came the ark containing the book of our sacred constitution; then a sarcophagus, surrounded with cypress and covered with crape, enclosing the ashes of the unfortunate National Guards killed at Nancy. A tall banner, adorned with mourning colours, bore in large letters the sad inscription, " *The victims of Bouillé.*" A band of music accompanied this, playing appropriate airs. Great numbers of National Guards mingled with the citizens, marching in the order of the procession, and holding each other by the arm : a few women were with them. No constituted body was assembled there, but I distinguished individually Danton, Manuel, Santerre, &c., &c. The soldiers of Château Vieux walked in company with the National Guards and other soldiers. Wherever they passed they were greeted with a burst of applause. Women and children held out their arms to them ; men waved their hats, and rent the air with unanimous cries of " *Long live Château Vieux!*" " *Long live the Nation!*" " *Long live Liberty !* "

But now another and equally interesting spectacle

changed the sentiment of the moment, and gave us new pleasure, mixed with tender compassion. A galley with oars, carried on a high car, and bearing the inscription " *The crime, not the scaffold, makes the shame !* " was followed by a hundred young ladies, dressed like nymphs, and quite as lovely, carrying the chains of the unhappy soldiers. This brilliant cortége was terminated by a sarcophagus with inscriptions in honour of the soldiers so inhumanly sentenced by the court-martial, and forty young girls carrying small banners with the name of one of those soldiers of Château Vieux who had escaped the vengeance of the court, inscribed on each. The flags of the three free nations floated, interlaced by a tri-coloured garland. I do not put everything exactly in its order, and I am sure to forget something, for I have not yet read any account of the *fête,* and all this I observed for myself. The eighty-three departments were represented by eighty-three men, each man carrying a tri-coloured banner with the name of his department; and then there were more groups of National Guards, citizens, porters from the Halles in their costumes, &c.

As there were gaps here and there in the procession, to give this great mass time to unite, groups of dancers filled them, and danced to the air of *Ça ira,* which was sung by the spectators at the windows. Although not in the programme, the dance was very animated, and formed one of the chief beauties of the *fête.* The procession was more

than an hour in passing, and afforded during the
whole time the most varied and picturesque of
spectacles. The applause, and the shouts in honour
of liberty, were unanimously repeated with such
touching enthusiasm that no music could be more
delightful to listen to. But now give all your attention to the magnificent car that approaches, drawn
by twenty white horses, adorned with the constitutional colours, led by men wearing the red cap, who
walked beside the horses to prevent accidents.
Two or three men sat in the lower part of the car,
and one only held the reins. The car was a double
structure ; the seats, empty, but prettily decorated,
did not look bad, though they had been intended
for something else. Fame, represented by the
statue of a beautiful woman, was placed at the top,
with an inscription that I could not make out. The
proud statue of Liberty was on the platform of the
car, accompanied by the horn of plenty and all the
attributes of glory and happiness. The bas-reliefs
were magnificent, the enthusiasm was indescribable,
and shouts of " Long live Liberty ! " " Liberty or
death ! " were so continually repeated that I seem
to hear them still. At eight o'clock at night the
fête came to an end, after a complete success, and
the most perfect tranquillity.

Our worthy Pétion is covered with glory. He
had been wise enough to induce both the department
and the municipality to adopt the plan of leaving
the people to themselves, and trusting the good

order and peace of the day to their management. There was not one patrol or armed National Guard, either in the procession or in the streets, and yet in the midst of six hundred thousand people no one was inconvenienced. Good nature is the people's police. I was there; and that my good sister Virginie, whose absence I much regretted, may not think that my patriotism exaggerates anything, tell her that if there was another *fête* to-morrow I should not be afraid to send Auguste to it alone, so much was I struck by the politeness and good order I saw everywhere to-day.

The best of it all is that the schemers failed. I shall mention no names, but you will recognize them all. The mother of a certain commandant besought me to shut myself up in the house with my family. Her son had told her the troops were assembled and in readiness at headquarters, that they would force Pétion to hoist the red flag, and that the streets would be swept of all the foolish people who wanted *fêtes* by the fatal *mitraille* of the canon. M. B—— (an artist from Desisle, who went some time ago to Nancy to paint a national picture for a pendant to David's "Jeu de paume") told me, in an interesting conversation I had with him, some amazing things he had heard from the father and mother of that young hero who was killed by the soldiers of his regiment. The Château Vieux were then out of the town.

The excess of my joy is in proportion to my

dread that there would have been bloodshed to-day.

XIX.

To her Husband.

Paris, *April* 20, 1792.

All Paris is at the National Assembly to-day. Jules, who had got ten deputies' cards and the twelve of your gallery, made a very agreeable distribution of them. Our good Abbé S—— had his share. He went there at half-past seven this morning, and assured us when he came back that the crowd was so great that not half would find places. The king is coming to-day to announce the war. Jules has kept his journal regularly since you left, and for the rest of the time his pen is never out of his hand. He wanted to take me with him to the Assembly this morning, but my hope of having a letter, and the new system we have adopted to make Auguste work, were two powerful reasons for depriving myself of that pleasure. I have not left my nest once all the week. I have heard a report that the paper money is falling rapidly.

The Assembly was so tremendously full of people to-day, that the sitting was closed immediately after the king went away. His speech, demanding the war, was simple and constitutional ; the answer of the President was laconic and just. The sitting was closed before two o'clock : the deputies were annoyed by the number of women who were allowed to penetrate even into the sanctuary. This, my dear husband, is what Jules tells me : he is at present writing in his room. The debates will begin to-morrow, and will be of such intense interest that we shall doubly regret your absence.

The *Moniteur* of to-day, dating from Frankfort on the 14th, announces that they have received news of the arrest and imprisonment of the Empress of Russia. It is quite true that the King of Sweden is dead : the Elector of Mayence is very ill. There seems to be so general a mortality amongst those who are the most exasperated at the French Revolution, that I believe still more firmly in my Divine Providence which works so miraculously. I have but one little scruple, like the good Suisse when he approached the holy table, I am afraid that, after a victory, of which I will not admit a doubt, our chiefs will turn their guns against certain decrees which seem to emanate directly from Providence— they are so wise and just. If these leaders were of our opinion, this war would be, in less than two months, the surest means of securing a certain and universal peace.

M. Gouvion has sent in his resignation as deputy, and has had the letter he wrote to the President published in the papers. He says he cannot any longer take his seat amongst colleagues who have awarded honours to his brother's assassins, &c., &c. M. Moi, curé of St. Laurent, has taken his place. I leave you to your reflections on this resignation and its motives. As for me, I am so sad, so grieved, so spiritless, that I have not two ideas in my head.

XX.

TO HER HUSBAND.

PARIS,
April 20 (fourth year), 1792.

M. de Semonville's adventure with the court of Savoy has made a great sensation.

I should like well enough to talk politics with you, but the rumours of war silence me, and our miserable internal dissensions grieve me so profoundly that I prefer to say nothing. Public confidence and patriotic energy are, however, so strong, that the Bourse, the thermometer of a good many people, is marvellously prosperous. All securities are rising. As for the National Assembly, it rings with the renown of patriotic gifts, and it is no longer the Rhine, as a certain deputy said, that rolls its waves through the Riding School, separating the right from the left, but the Pactolus. Let those who thirst for gold beware lest they be drowned in it! The desks of the secretaries are laden with heaps of gold at every sitting. This passionate generosity must make our enemies tremble, and is a truly Roman proof of the elevation of the public spirit. I may just as well gossip about nothing as talk politics, because I must not say everything, nor call things by their names. There is so much underhand work, there are so many intrigues and such singular projects afoot, that none can foresee the *dénouement* of all this. But mere human prudence will once more be disconcerted, for Providence is there, and ready to work one of those miracles which confound the boldest.

An apple of discord has been flung among the Jacobins. Collot has denounced Rœderer and Brissot, and Robespierre has sent in his resignation as public accuser; all this is talked of in whispers.

As there are no dykes powerful enough to check the revolutionary spirit which philosophy has breathed into the whole of Europe, let us expect great things. Our little vagaries of sentiment are trifles of the human mind, that will not hinder the accomplishment of great events. Reflect for an instant on Robespierre's character, and consider the motives of this step of his. I fancy you will find out the *why* immediately, if you can only discover whom they were that waved the magic wand which has given us a Jacobin ministry. That is not clear, but guess, and let us talk of other things. . . . .

XXI.

To her Husband.

Paris,
Whit-Sunday (fourth year), 1792.

I went to-day to the National Assembly to get the tickets M. D—— had promised me. He gave me five for Auguste and myself. They are not of

much use to me, for I can always get in, when I
do not arrive too late. The miracles of the revolutionary Providence begin to manifest themselves.
I never was at a more interesting sitting, and I
never saw more admirable unity of action. They are
afraid, yet they display the most intrepid firmness.
The Senate is declared permanent. It paused
neither day nor night in its efforts to save the
common weal, now in imminent danger. Gensonné,
Bazire, Brissot, Merlin, Chabot, Carnot, and Isnard,
have each proved the conspiracy, by isolated facts;
but the general report and the proof are to be
presented to-morrow night and the following days,
until everything has been perfectly cleared up. The
prelude occurred to-day. The municipality of
Neuilly sent to the National Assembly a handful
of white cockades, that had been torn from the
Swiss Guards by the peasants at a *fête champêtre*
which took place yesterday. The Swiss Guards
drew their swords, cursed the nation and insulted
the constitution. Our brave peasants held their
ground, the authorities did wonders, and the account
of the affair, read in the Senate, let in the light of
truth on the malevolence of the Swiss Guards, who
were arrested, but afterwards given up to their
colonel. All this is sharply criticized. A despatch
has arrived from the municipality of St. Cloud,
stating that M. de la Porte, intendant of the Civil
List, went to the porcelain manufactory followed
by a vehicle laden with fifty-two bales. He had

the furnaces lighted, and all the bales burned in them.

He was brought to the bar, and appeared with a guilty face. I believe he tells the most brazen lies, but thanks to the ability of the President he got off scot free. He says that the papers destroyed were some thousands of copies of the " Life of Mme. Lamotte." He was asked the name of the printer, who is ordered to appear, as are also the persons employed in the factory; but they live so far away that they did not arrive in time for me to hear them. M. Servan, Minister of War, spoke. The scene changed, and other dangers were disclosed. The refusal three years ago, to arm the National Guards residing on the frontier, exposes them without defence to the fury of the enemy. The minister asked for prompt measures to remedy this act of perfidy, and spoke so forcibly about the guilty negligence of his predecessors that his speech elicited loud applause. It is to be printed, and a report will be made to-morrow, and followed by a decree. M. Servan propounded an idea that you have often expressed; it is that voluntary troops should be organized in each department, under the command of a retired officer of the line, the other officers to be drawn from their ranks. These troops should be drilled and put through their exercises every Sunday morning in each chief place. Bazire, Lacroix, and Isnard have denounced the King's Guard and demanded its suppression. They affirm

F

that refractory priests, lackeys, and officers from Coblentz are included in it.

Orgies are beginning again, as scandalous as those of Versailles. The healths of Condé and Bouillé are drank. The national cockade is trampled underfoot, and so on. An unfortunate man, one of the King's Guard, was nearly murdered by his comrades for drinking the health of the " Prince royal " instead of the " Dauphin," but the others interfered in time. Bazire, who supplied all these details, says he had them from some brave body-guards who were there only by accident. The protection of the law was claimed for them. I expect they will appear at the bar. Chabot said he had 180 written testimonies, and that the citizens, weary of being accused of calumny, had offered to come and maintain their signatures. Montmorin has fled, and now do you doubt the existence of the Austrian Committee? we have never doubted it, and you, dear husband, in your speech at Voiron, prophesied exactly all that is now taking place. But one is never a prophet in one's own country. If you had been in the National Assembly the evil would not have reached such a height, because your uprightness and clearsighted-ness would have secured numerous partisans for you. Half the Assembly is composed of men who are weak and blind, and who are glad to avail themselves of a sure support when they can lay hold on me.

Gaudet spoke like a Roman; so did Kersaint, the younger Carnot, and La Source. The opposition looked utterly foolish and mean. They are so well acquainted with the plot for the re-establishment of the nobility and the two Chambers, that it is believed several amongst them are already named dukes and peers. This alarms us considerably; Paris is full of people from Coblentz, and most of the officers of our National Guard are aristocrats. Pétion has to come to the bar every morning to give an account of the police arrangements of the capital. He has been advised to double the guards in the evening and during the night.

The king's letter against this brave magistrate is a masterpiece of the royal bad faith. The mayor's answer is in the simple language of truth and virtue. Some people are quite the opposite of those virtues, and if the terrible plot had not created such a disturbance, our dear Pétion would have run the risk of being assassinated. His was the first head to be demanded.

Servan drew a lamentable picture of some sixty leagues of our frontiers which are entirely unprotected. Lacoste's turn came then. He said the navy was completely disorganized, and that, if prompt measures were not taken, the evil would soon be irremediable. If these two ministers had meant to discourage every one they could not have adopted a better plan, for just now the public mind, full of distrust, dreads everything. The pleasure I

had in listening to these speeches is considerably
diminished by reflection.   So many and such
urgent reforms seem beyond human power and
are enough to appal the strongest minds; but
the energetic resolution to have permanent sittings,
and not to take one moment of repose till the crisis
is over, shows that there is as much courage as
danger.   Duranton, Minister of Justice, does the
same as Duport-Dutertre.   Decidedly the air of the
court is pestilential.   Duranton, who comes from
Bordeaux, was once as philosophical as Cincinnatus,
but now, drawn from his profound retirement, he
has become a courtier as well as a minister.   I cannot get over it, and therefore I no longer believe in
any civic virtues but yours.   Adieu!

XXII.

To her Husband.

Paris, *April* 30, 1792.

Ah, my dear husband, how I have wished for you
these last three days!   It would require the pen of
Tacitus to write their history.   Never, no, never,
have the people shown themselves more calm or
more powerful, and, to the eyes of a philosopher and
observer, the splendour of their majesty is far more
imposing than that of any king.   I saw the Tuileries,
the Courts of the Château, and the neighbourhood
of the Senate filled with a crowd of from two to
three hundred thousand people, and yet not a foot

was trodden on. The people had truly risen, and
stood erect in their pride and their might. You
never saw anything approaching it since the Revolution, and to think that our eyes beheld this
great sight! I wanted to cross the Tuileries last
Tuesday on coming out of the National Assembly,
and I thought I should never be able to get through.
I went to each of the four gates, but could not get
out, and the garden was completely filled, as were
also the great Courts of the Château. Crossing
above them, I saw the lion's-den well guarded on
every side; the crowd was quite dense from there
to the Pont-Neuf. Marion, who had also gone to
the Tuileries, had squeezed herself into several of
the groups and heard many excellent things. The
people are proud of their strength, and will not
abuse it. Numerous patrols circulated in the crowd,
but respected their moderation, and saw nothing to
check or punish. I stayed at the Assembly on
Tuesday from eight in the morning until five in the
evening. The interest of the sitting increased at
every instant up to the crowning-point, as though
Providence had composed, for this particular day, a
grand tragedy, the excitement and importance
increasing with every scene. The people's magistrate, Pétion, came to give an account of the
Parisian police. His speech was eloquent and
simple. " The most perfect calm reigns under the
protection of unrelaxed vigilance. The legislator
may raise himself to the height at which the will of

the people has placed him, without fear that his
deliberations will be disturbed by any disorder.
The mass of the citizens of this vast capital is pure,
their civic spirit is firm and enlightened, the
malevolent will not dare to show themselves,"
&c., &c. All this was received with clapping
of hands, shouts of "bravo," and a delirium
of joy sufficient to split the arched roof of the
temple. The mayor crossed the hall to the
sound of the sincerest and most enthusiastic
applause. About twenty *invalides* presented themselves at the bar, and nobly expressed their
regret for the painful obligation that they were
under, to denounce their officers on account of the
orders they had received during the night. These
orders were to open the gates to the King's Guards,
even to the National Guards. The utterances of
these brave soldiers drew tears from our eyes. The
officers were called to the bar. To shorten my story,
I may tell you, here, that they got themselves cleverly
out of the difficulty by saying they apprehended a
disturbance in Paris during the night, and had
given those orders so as to insure the safety of
all who should take refuge in their own houses.
Weigh and judge that excuse in your wisdom.
They have been dismissed. Bazire began his
denunciation of the King's Guards; his introductory
speech was short and moderate. The reading of
the papers authentically signed lasted two hours,
and even then they left more than they had read

from distaste to the subject, and because the proofs
of the offences were more than sufficient. Three
young guards asked to be heard at the bar, and in
the language of free and candid minds they denounced the horrors of which they had been the
witnesses and the victims, having been exposed on
account of their civic spirit to every sort of oppression. They said that in the queen's antechamber
the defeat of Mons was looked upon as a glorious
success. " Three hundred *sans - culottes* have
perished already : bravo ! Let the earth be purged
of this vermin, and our master will be king," &c., &c.
My pen refuses to write what I have heard. The
ferocity of tigers is the humanity of courts. The
discussion was opened. Dumas dared to defend the
King's Guards. Others, more adroitly, invoked the
constitution to prevent their being disbanded according to Bazire's demand. Some military music
that we heard at that moment rested our minds
after a discussion that was becoming stormy. All
was miraculous in that sitting ; the succession of
incidents caused one to pass by degrees through
the different feelings of horror, pity, admiration, joy,
pleasure, and pain. We felt them all by turns, and
with a force aroused by the most intense interest and
the most terrible danger.

The military music announced the section of the
Gobelins and the Faubourg St. Marceau. The
orator, who was in rags, spoke like Cicero ; I do
not know where he found such great beauties of

eloquence, but none could be more striking. The
orator entreated the Assembly to permit the honest
citizens of the section to pass through the hall, that
the legislators might see how many hearts were
devoted to them, and how many hands carried arms
to support them.   Six thousand people; soldiers,
men, women, and children, passed through in a new
and striking order.   The groups of citizens were
divided at regular distances by two or three ranks
of soldiers, and all marched to the sound of a drum
beaten in quick time.   The women held their
right arms aloft, the men were armed with pikes,
pitchforks, and tridents, which were intermingled
with the bayonets of the soldiers.   The children
held drawn swords in their hands, and the hall resounded with cries of " *Liberty or death—Constitution or death !* "   " *Long live the National Assembly.
Down with tyrants.*"   " *The French people are free ;
they have no longer any master but the law.*"   "*Long
live the law !* "   " *Long live the nation !*"   And this
lasted half-an-hour, during which time the applause
and the bravos made music a thousand times pleasanter
to the ear than all the harmonies of the opera.   Do
you not think, my dear husband, that Providence
itself devised this demonstration to stimulate the
courage of our deputies ?   The Blacks were turned
white by the virtue of fear, which is the only virtue
they possess, except the courage of shame.   They
were livid, and looked like fools.   In the evening the
Faubourg St. Antoine repeated the proceedings of

the Faubourg St. Marceau, which I have just described to you. The night passed in perfect quiet. Paris is carefully lighted, and the legislators, imperatively directed by public opinion, voted during the night the disbandment of that Pretorian Guard that was ready to cut our throats at the least sign. Brissac-Cossé was arrested by a vote of accusation, and taken to Orleans this morning. I longed and wished for you, my husband. These great scenes exhaust one. The danger we have been in, the insolence of the aristocrats, who proclaim the counter-revolution and a rain of blood, as one would foretell a salutary storm of rain; all this must have angered the Supreme Being, and I look upon all that has just happened as so many miracles of His power and goodness towards the people. Men have had little to do in it. The crimes were accumulated, the circumstances were developed and collected together by the Providence of the Revolution, without any help from human prudence, and this has forced the legislators to save us and themselves. *Suprema lex salus populi.*

XXIII.

To her Husband.

Paris,
May 3 (fourth year of liberty), 1792.

My dear husband, I throw myself into your arms, sad and weary, and not knowing what I may say to you safely. We are breathlessly waiting for news;

all hearts are troubled, all minds are on the strain, and everybody runs about to question everybody else. You know of Dillon's defeat, and his unhappy fate. A second engagement before Mons, under M. de Biron, has been equally unlucky, but he retreated in good order. This morning M. Truffer came to tell me that General de Biron has taken Mons, that the post had arrived at nine o'clock last night, and that he had his information from a sure source. We shall get the confirmation of it to-day. We are alarmed for the National Assembly. It is easy to see that it is bewildered with the noise of the canon, and the people are not satisfied with it. Our aristocrats exhibit an atrocious joy, which will I hope be of short duration.[1] In a word, dear husband, the Jacobin ministry makes us tremble, and if Providence does not strike a great blow our case will be pitiful. Suspicion is so strongly justified by treason, that it will require a miracle to make us victorious. I expect one from La Fayette, because his interests and ours are identical at this moment. He must invest himself with great confidence and power ; and all he is doing now tends to that.

Patience and courage ! We are in a state of con-

[1] The exultation of the French of the interior, the enemies of the Revolution, who openly placed their hopes in the success of the enemies from without, and in the armed occupation of French territory by the soldiers of the coalition, explains and justifies the popular and general indignation that broke out at a later period.

sternation, but hope saves us from utter prostration. If our Senate would only second public opinion, all this would be nothing. Mirabeau was right; the attention that must be given to war absorbs every mind, and that is a misfortune when there are so many other things to be done.

What abominable secrets will escape the publicity of history, and how monstrously wicked our nobles were and are! How happy you are to be away from it all. I fancy the trumpet of war does not prevent you from listening to the pastoral flute, and that my little sisters laugh and run about as if we were in a time of peace.

M. J——, who was careful not to give his vote to the new Public Accuser, told us of the storm raised by that nomination. It is incredible. We, that is, your children and I, feel that in spite of strong reasons for disgust and indignation, Robespierre ought to have kept his place, that he has been false to great principles, and that the people's magistrate should die at his post.

I think it fortunate that our good Pétion was able to conjure all the Jacobin storms, by a speech so full of wisdom that they passed to the order of the day on all the denunciations. Yes; but the leaven of discord is still fermenting. However, quiet reigns, and the great interest unites all.

I am making careful preparations for our dear son's departure to England. His letters of introduction will keep him waiting till the fifteenth; after that date, there will be no more hindrances on our side. I am embarrassed about his passport, and my mind is not easy, nor is my heart at rest; but I try to act prudently, and, I hope, to do my best. I am much pleased with Jules' conduct; he is always writing either in his own room or in the reporters' gallery. It is quite a passion with him. I embrace you tenderly, my dear husband : I love you as never woman loved before, and but for this accursed war I would write you volumes of tenderness. I shall lose all my credit with Mdlle. Virginie, if she remembers that 1 prophesied victory. But I look at the thing on the large scale, and consider it as a whole. We expected treason and little defeats; but it is when I think of the hecatombs of victims who are immolated to perfidy and intrigue, that I chiefly grieve for the war.

XXIV.

To her Husband.

PARIS, *May* 10, 1792.

Our eldest son has received letters from Messieurs Pétion, Dumouriez, Condorcet, and Sillery, containing letters of introduction for London. M. Dumouriez assures Jules, in two friendly letters, that if he remains in the ministry, Jules shall have a place as Secretary of Legation, which he would have given him six weeks ago if he had applied to him. About twenty deputies, and amongst them M. Hérault, have recommended him, and done all they can to procure acquaintances for him in London. He starts on Wednesday, and I am glad of it, though it wrings my heart to part with him. The places in the diligence to Calais are in such demand that I have only been able to secure one by a piece of good luck. All the seats were taken for the next fortnight, but at my request the clerk looked again through his register, and found that one traveller had altered his day of departure. This left one place free, for Wednesday the 16th. When you receive my letter we shall be shedding our farewell tears. You are happy with your philosophy, you get all the roses off your rosebushes, and the thorns are for the tender mother ; but that is woman's usual fate.

Do not be afraid of the Savoyard wren—he tries to act like the Austrian eagle ; all that cannot last long. Here I am talking politics without meaning it. I shrink with alarm from what I see in all this. They are fighting the Jacobins, and our simpletons are again becoming all they were before. The apple of discord has been cleverly thrown into the midst of society, and the beginning of the war with the Foreign Powers has been so arranged, that the Jacobin ministry gets all the blame of it. M. de Grave has sent in his resignation, M. Servan is in his place. (You find these Dauphinois everywhere.) M. de Grave is a mystery. I wonder what evil genius it is that renders everything mysterious to all but the small number of sensible persons who know what they are about, while the general public

is caught like a fish on a hook.   A petition against
the Jacobins, signed by 30,000 of these simpletons
(*badauds*) is to be presented to the National Assembly next Sunday.   Every one is full of it, and
Vaublanc, Jaucourt, Chéron, &c., are waiting to
support it with their usual zeal for everything good.
Devils of every hue are arriving in Paris from all
parts of the country.   It is thought there will be
some disturbance.   Our National Guard is not
favourably disposed towards what we call "*the
flower of the patriots,*" or what the court calls the
Republicans.   "That is a faction that must be
crushed, for it is opposed to the reign of the law."
Foolish speeches like these abound in the constitutional region, which looks for stars at midday.   Such
strange blindness confounds all human reason.
Nothing is talked of but the petition.   War, politics,
everything is neglected.   The Jacobins, the Jacobins; nothing but the Jacobins!   The storm is so
violent that it alarms the most courageous.   Their
letters are intercepted, and the thread of their correspondence is broken.   Every crime is permitted
that may lead to that one which would fill up the
measure of our wrongs.   They want to arrive at
destroying the protection societies, which have succeeded by their watchfulness in defeating all the
plans of our treacherous enemies.   Then they will
only have to draw in the net—we shall all be taken.
Sensible people are furious; but things have been so
cleverly managed that the fools are imposed on.

Society has been divided, and is rent asunder by its own act. The partisans of war on the offensive method dispute with those who were against it, and who had prophesied all that has happened. Robespierre and Brissot, the two heads of the opposing parties, have each their partisans, so war is raging in society with as much violence as on the frontiers, and is bringing us to the edge of the precipice. My thoughts are consequently gloomy, and were it not for the miracles I expect from Divine Providence, which has up to the present confounded all human powers, I hardly know what I should think. The indifference, the selfishness, the base personal interest that I see everywhere cause me the deepest distress. I remember now your fatal prophecies, and they go to my heart. I am as much grieved, as much vexed, and as stupid as it is possible to be. Will the National Assembly ruin France after having saved her? We cannot say now, as formerly : the provinces will raise their voice; for the departments and the municipalities often suppress public opinion, that they may manifest only their own. The diversity of feeling in the good party is quite incredible. The other goes straighter to the point, for the excellent reason that to the powerful and the wicked all means are good. I will say no more, for you are better acquainted with the subject than I am. Jules is strongly recommended to Lord Stanhope and to the Bishop of Autun. The note M. Pétion wrote to him ac-

companying a letter of introduction was very kind,
although short. Perlet is pleading the Jacobins'
cause to-night admirably. Advocates for and
against it will not be wanting. They pretend that
the post suppresses all the good newspapers, and
complaints are made on every side. The enforced
idleness of our troops makes my blood boil: it
looks as if they were giving the others time to beat
us. Everything is going on as badly as possible.

XXV.

TO HER HUSBAND.

PARIS, *May* 16, 1792.

Messieurs Dumouriez, Condorcet, La Rochefoucauld, and Brissot warmly approve the plan of sending Jules to London. The poor child is provided
with so many letters of introduction that he will be
too busy when he gets there. He has letters for
Dr. Priestley, Lord Stanhope, Talleyrand, Chauvelin
the ambassador, young Garat, &c. The letter I
prize most is that of Mme. Le Roux to her brother,
M. de Meuse, asking him to keep Jules at his house
for the first few days, and to treat him as his own
son.

I started him off this morning. Mmes. Déjean
and Perrond went with me. We were all three
miserable, and Jules went away overwhelmed with
our caresses and touched by our regret. I inspected
his travelling-companions. There was a Dutchman,

a genuine patriot, who told us in two words, with the straightforward brevity of a thinker, that he would take care of Jules, and give him help and good advice if it were necessary. The storm lowers here. The talk of plots and assassinations, a sort of St. Bartholomew of patriots, makes me tremble. The truth is, things are going ill, and our enemies seem triumphant. I am sick with anxiety; and when I see the other side of the medal I am glad of your absence. I say in my heart: is this, too, a favour of Providence?

XXVI.

To her Son.

PARIS, *May* 19, 1792.

I should like to talk politics with you, but I have such gloomy views on the subject that I am afraid to reveal them. Carra has been brought before the magistrates by Montmorin and Bertrand (noxious animals that they are!). He said he had had his notes from Bazire, Merlin, and Chabot. The magistrates presented themselves at the Assembly to claim the papers: they passed to the order of the day. Bazire said it was in the interests of the nation, the king, and the queen, that they should remain buried in oblivion; which, to those who have ears to hear, means that all our enemies are in the same nest —the court. Since the most criminal indulgence is extended to it, can one expect anything but misfortune? I should at least have liked to deliver

Carra from the grip of chicanery, but the order of the day, supported by Dumolard, has left innocence oppressed, and suffered crime to go free. It is but the repetition of the scenes you have had before your eyes for the last two months. Our Assembly is either cowardly or corrupt. I can think nothing good of it. The inaction of our troops confirms the ideas of those who suspect the existence of a great treasonable combination by all the constituted authorities, to hinder or destroy a state of things which displeases the ambitiously powerful as well as the vicious rich.

I had a long letter from your father yesterday. He is at Grenoble, and tells me they are making a fortified town of it, with a camp in the environs, and that the peasants burn with patriotic zeal.

I went with Mdlle. C—— to the sermon at St. Eustache. Never, no never, has the pulpit of truth been so worthily filled. The preacher delivered a brilliant discourse on the means of preventing civil war, and turning the war with the Foreign Powers all to our advantage. He held both the New Testament and the Constitution in his hand, and preached the reign of Liberty, Equality, and Fraternity with all the power of genius. He drew striking and truthful pictures of the wickedness of tyrants and courts, and of the degradation and misery of the people; indeed I have not read anything so fine or so forcible since the Revolution. His skilful contrast of this state of things with the reign of a citizen-king, who, faithful to his oath, would tread firmly in the path of virtue, raising himself with the nation to the height of glory, was touchingly and magnificently ironical. Neither Fléchier nor Bourdaloue ever had such a splendid triumph. At the moment when, in a sublime burst of eloquence, he called down the lightnings of divine justice on the heads of the guilty, a real clap of thunder shook the arched roof of the church. Roman superstition would have augured from such a sign that Jupiter was favourable. We admired in silence the singular and fortunate coincidence, and in the depths of our hearts we all implored the Divinity to manifest His justice and power with a like terrible might. The audience were so charmed and delighted with this worthy minister of the Supreme Being, that they applauded him again and again.

After the sermon we went to the Tuileries, where we found everything in an uproar in consequence of Carra's story, which has produced a remarkable effect. The magistrate, emboldened by the order of the day that had protected his first infringement of the laws in the attack on Carra, had had the audacity to issue a warrant for his arrest, and to have it executed. At five o'clock, Saturday morning, five *sbirri* of the National Gendarmerie dragged Merlin out of bed to lead him before Etienne Rivière, the magistrate of the Henri IV. section. There he was interrogated, &c., &c. You can imagine, my son, all the complaints that this popular deputy had the

right to make to the Senate, of which he is a member.
The " blacks " had the meanness openly to oppose
their colleagues, who had been so shamefully treated.
After a frightful tumult the majority prevailed : the
magistrate was called to the bar, arrested, and sent
to Orleans.   This makes the wicked intentions of the
court quite clear ; one must be blind not to see that
the plot was on the point of execution ; but it was
necessary to paralyze the patriotic newspapers by
some salient measure, and to terrorize the incorruptible deputies. Divine justice has permitted all this to
turn to their own shame ; and the king has addressed
to the Assembly a letter as awkward as it is impolitic.
The people howl with indignation, but obedience
to the law restrains them.

   They talk here of a victory of the English over
Tippoo Sahib, which will put them in possession of
all the wealth of Hindoostan. Tell me if this be true ?
I am interested in all that concerns that nation.   I
was filled with admiration on reading the discussion
on the slave-trade ; I shall continue to follow the
progress of that great matter, which is the business
of all humanity.   Do not forget to tell me the
general opinion of our Revolution. Great good may
perhaps spring from the excess of our ills.   Here
we are awaiting some great event. The Jacobins
have recovered their calm in the midst of the
tempests that threaten them. A great deal of nonsense is talked about the evils unjustly attributed
to them.   Carra's affair has so unexpectedly roused

the patriotic spirit that I hope sincerely it will turn to
the advantage of the Jacobins, who are in general the
flower of patriotism. While I am writing, they are
calling out in the streets : " Discovery of an infernal
plot of the Feuillants; innocence of the Jacobins
recognized." I do not offer you advice as to your
conduct : I have the proud confidence that in giving
up my son to himself I leave him in the hands of a
strict and enlightened judge; but I must remind
you of one thing that will keep that inflexible judge,
your conscience, ever awake and watchful. It is
that one fault of youth blights every age in a man's
life; whereas the teachings of virtue, steadily and
faithfully followed, fill the soul with joy, and cover
the most rugged paths of life with flowers. I know
of but one durable beauty, but one solid good; I
see but one means of happiness—virtue. All the
rest is delusion.

You know my profound veneration for Dr.
Priestley. If you are lucky enough to see him,
regard him as if he were Phocion, Aristides, or
Socrates resuscitated; he is a great man, and his
wisdom will stand comparison with anything you
have read of the three others. I long for your
opinion on a thousand things; go a little more into
details, and don't jump over so many circumstances.

Our patriotic papers revive one's courage by their
high and energetic tone. The Commune, and no
doubt the Jacobins, have deliberated all night.
Opposite our door this morning a cart was stopped;

it was filled with specie, packed in little barrels; the people and the gendarmes took it back to the city. Almost all the news indicates a general ferment, the result of which is still hidden in the urn of destiny; I think, however, that it has defeated the great conspiracy. We breathe and hope. Love your mother tenderly, Jules, and think of her every minute.

XXVII.

PARIS, *May* 23, 1792.

Man proposes and God disposes. There was such a crowd at the Assembly yesterday that I could not find a place. Every spot was crammed, and patriotism shone in every eye. Brissot and Gensonné made splendid speeches in proof of the existence of the Austrian Committee. I suppose you learn all that goes on here from the newspapers, so I pass over details. It is as clear to me as that two and two make four, that the story of Carra, Merlin, Bazire, and Chabot has defeated a barbarous plot that was on the point of being put into execution, and which would have cost the life and liberty of the flower of our patriots. The stupid crowd asks for material proofs, and it is impossible to obtain anything but moral certainty, because all evil geniuses are clever and prudent enough to concoct their crimes in secret, without leaving traces that may serve to convict them. They say, however, that the two speeches carry clear evidence with them. The conclusion has been adjourned to Friday : then we shall see. God protects us, and our enemies in their mad presumption betray their plots by the most insulting joy. They think themselves sure of victory before the battle, and, for some time, nothing can exceed the proud hopes they manifest. They have still many chances in their favour ; but the people are on the alert, and Heaven prepares some new miracle in our favour.

We went back to the Tuileries at about six o'clock : all Paris was assembled there, in numerous groups. We witnessed two incidents which violently excited the crowd. An officer struck a colporteur because he was selling "The justification of the Jacobins." He would have been maltreated by the crowd had it not been for the National Guards, who, while they blamed the officer, promised the people that justice should be done. But even as it was, he was shaken, beaten, hissed, and conducted to the guard-house by two or three thousand people. I was sitting on the parapet of the terrace by the waterside, and witnessed the whole scene, which occurred between the terrace of the Feuillants and the palace-gates. It was as if I were on a rock in the midst of a raging sea. No sooner was quiet restored than the storm recommenced. Human waves were rolling in every direction. The poet Roucher wanted to harangue a group, and they were trying to plunge him in the basin of the fountain to cool his aristoçratic zeal. Fortunately a magistrate showed his little white wand to the crowd, and the good people, struck by the sudden appearance of the symbol of the law which they all desire to respect, contented themselves with insisting that Roucher should be turned out of the Tuileries garden; so two or three thousand of them followed him to the gates near the Pont Royal. There I saw the crowd disperse, and I went away, so as to get home by daylight. I assure you patriotism is roused, but its enemies are so cunning and so powerful, that it will have to fight more than one battle before the victory can be gained.

Food has doubled in price, every means is employed to weary and exhaust the people. M. Euvy told me that a great many Jacobins had been maltreated at the Tuileries last night. He said he had attended a meeting of the Jacobins, where he had heard a terrible denunciation of La Fayette, based on a letter from I don't know where, which affirms that the general has given up the offensive war and is keeping simply on the defensive. Can that be possible? If so, it is certain that the diversity of opinion on the subject of the general will lead to a war in society. He has so many friends, and so many enemies, that the public good is forgotten in thinking only of the individual. This is a miserable fact.

XXVIII.

Paris, *June* 1, 1792.

A dream, a nothing, frightens us when those we love are in question. My son, I dreamed last night that your brother, you, and I, were walking together by the pale uncertain light of the moon on the edge of a precipice. As I know of nothing better than coolness and intrepidity in danger, I said to you courageously, "Let us walk carefully, my children; but let us walk." You made a false step which precipitated you before my eyes to a hundred feet below. I called for help, and lay down on the almost perpendicular rock; then sliding rapidly downwards I reached the bottom almost as soon as yourself; I lifted you up, all bruised, but full of life and courage. Two men who had followed me, took you in their arms, and carried you up so steep a path that the foot of man had never before trodden it. I walked with difficulty behind the group—maternal love gave me the strength of Hercules—and at last the joy of reaching the top woke me up, covered with perspiration and panting with relief. This dream had so agitated me that I could not go to sleep again. Is it prophetic? What danger threatens you? My dear child, I always see you walking among the volcanoes, the precipices, the abysses of the passions of your age. Think what my reflections must be!

I implore you, in your mother's name, to watch over my son.

I again repeat the advice I have already given you. Let your conscience, with wise suspicion, watch over every step you take. How dear you are to me, my son, and what firm confidence I have in that natural love of goodness which I am sure education and the example of the best of fathers has strengthened in your soul. My darling, a dream is often but a lie, but a woman's imagination and a mother's heart are terrified at everything. I am waiting with impatience for your letter to come and banish my fears.

If you meet a Quaker anywhere, kiss the hem of his garment for me. In my opinion, among all the multitudes of men on the face of the earth there are none who do such honour to humanity. As I only know them by hearsay, tell me all about them if you meet any of them, and let me know whether Voltaire and the other philosophers have flattered them or not.

I am in your room, at your desk, my son; I almost fancy I am with your soul which reposed here while it was developing its first thoughts. I am sitting in your chair; everything around me reminds me of you, speaks to me of you, and more than all the rest, my heart identifies me, so to speak, with everything that has any connexion with my dear Jules. I am hoping that the post to-day will bring me a letter from you. I need one, to help

me to bear the double anxieties caused by the
absence of one dearest to me. The Holy Spirit has
indeed descended on the apostles of the constitution.
Whitsun-week was a real time of miracles. Providence has accumulated proofs of our enemies'
crimes, and has summoned them before the tribunal
of public opinion, with such evidence that the blind
see, the lame walk, and the friends of humanity
in both parties offer thanksgivings to Heaven, that
has saved the capital from the rain of blood with
which our enemies were ready to inundate it. Yes,
dear Jules, Paris would have been a prey to the
most horrible carnage if the King's Guard had not
been disbanded. It was the rallying-point. Twenty
thousand traitors, disguised as National Guards,
would have reinforced them to help in carrying off
the king, and would have drowned all who opposed
them in blood ! Poor people ! What a plaything
are you for the plots and intrigues of a perfidious
court !

During these two *fêtes* I have been at the
National Assembly, where I have seen and heard
everything, and the isolated proofs collected here
and there so remarkably support the official denunciation, that one must indeed be blind not to
discern at once the knot of the fatal conspiracy.
The results are, that Pétion behaved with the prudence and wisdom of a magistrate. Cicero did not
resist the Roman Catiline with more eloquence and
firmness than Pétion the French Catilines. The

King's Guard is broken up, their chief, Brissac, is at Orleans. The decrees were sanctioned as soon as presented, because the numberless crimes were proved beyond all dispute. The people had risen, and in that proud attitude they had struck down their enemies, without having the pain of fighting them. Their respect for the law has done wonders. I was at the Tuileries in the midst of fifty thousand people, and the majestic agitation we were all in did not cause the least disorder. On all sides was heard " Respect the law." " Obey the law." Heaven itself is in arms to punish the great crimes that have been committed. The pure and imposing mass of the nation affects our enemies like the head of Medusa. It astonishes and petrifies them. There has not been so much as a scratch in all Paris during these stormy days. By order of the magistrates, the people were charged with the watch, and the police regulations were confided to the National Guards, who did wonders. My timid neighbours think me very intrepid for daring to pass the threshold of my house, but, as I said to the Abbé, sensible people are not afraid when the right side is victorious; the real danger is when the other party gets the upper hand. For them, the worst means are good if they only lead to the object they have in view, whereas we employ justice, order, and peace only to attain ours.

The strongest party in France, stronger than all those who adopt the different names and signs of their factions, is composed of the imposing majority of the right-minded and single-hearted. These are they who judge men and even kings, who consult history, and examine the past as a guide for the future. These are they who think that the will of the nation is so strongly expressed in favour of the constitution, that that same constitution will exist throughout all ages. The constitution made by men, will in its turn make men, who, having nothing of the prejudices of their fathers, nor of the vices of the present age, will become its sure and stable support.

The Englishman I saw at M. C.'s assured me that it would not be safe for you to display your patriotic sentiments in London, so I beg you to be prudent and circumspect. Be sure not to show my letters, and put a padlock on your lips ; the foreigner should respect the hospitable country that receives him. I should be more anxious if you had less control over yourself, but your natural philanthropy, and the modesty proper to your age, are my securities for my son.

No news from the frontier. Your little brother made his patriotic gift. After having made his patriotic gift and his speech, he had the honours of the sitting, and with loud applause ! The "pious fury" which animates the public mind is so sustained that I do not exaggerate when I say it rains gold. Yesterday a Bordeaux man laid on the altar of the country 57,000 livres in coin, and every day the bureau is covered with gold.

Good-bye, dear child ; this is all you will get from me to-day, unless a nice letter comes to make me reopen my quiver. You know how fond I am of using my pen to talk with your papa and you. I saw in the *Moniteur* yesterday the answer of the King of England to the King of the French, and the proclamation for the maintenance of the treaty of commerce. All that is truly royal, &c., &c. I read attentively everything that relates to England. I think I am half-English ; why is there a camp near London ? I am frightened at everything, dear child. Liberty in its infancy is so easily startled. I pray God every day for the prosperity of the peoples, for it is in that caste, the oppressed of all time, that the virtues abide. I pray for you, also, my son : remember that the eye of the Supreme Being embraces all the universe, and is fixed on you, the august witness of all your actions.

We had a *fête* to-day in honour of the Mayor of Étampes, that might be called the *fête* of the law. There was a splendid procession ; all the Parisian troops were under arms ; the National Assembly, the municipality, the department, the ministers, and groups of citizens and citizenesses. The ceremony took place on the field of the Federation. I was not there. The mottoes were all in the same spirit. " *To be free we must be united.*" " *She strikes to defend herself.*" " *The law alone rules all.*" " *Free men are slaves of the law,*" &c. The *fête* came to an end amid the most perfect quiet ; and, though the

day was not very fine, and there was a slight storm
and some rain, the people who saw it told us that
everything went off as well as possible, and the
military music was most brilliant. It is seven
o'clock, and all is over; everybody is gone home.
Three camps are being made between Lyons and
Grenoble.

M. Servan, the minister, with whom we are inti-
mately acquainted, inspires us with great confidence.
You will see in the newspapers that the ministers'
salaries have been reduced to 50,000 francs, except
that of the Minister of Foreign Affairs. He has
75,000. Tell me what French papers you see in
London.

XXIX.

To her Husband.

Paris, *June* 6, 1792.

Jules did not see Lord Stanhope when he called
on him in London. My lord asked for his address
and went himself to see him at M. de Meuse's:
Jules was not at home. Lord Stanhope politely
asked Madame de Meuse to beg the young foreigner
to come to his house. They talked French together
for two hours, and the philosopher lord overwhelmed the poor child with attentions. The
Bishop of Autun has placed himself at his disposal.
M. Chauvelin received him most kindly, asked him
to come often, and the second time he went there
offered to send his letters with his own; he has

besides offered him a place in the ambassador's box
at all the theatres.

Mdme. D—— and your brother dined with me
yesterday. They are more aristocratic than ever,
see black where I see white, and white where I see
black ; and yet they pretend to love the people and
the public prosperity as sincerely and as warmly as
I do. It is a pity that the same source should produce two streams that flow in contrary directions.
We discussed without disputing ; we made war with
the olive-branch in our hands, and entrenched ourselves within the fortress of our consciences, which
made us so firm and obstinate in the diversity of
our opinions, that we each beat a retreat, attributing
to ourselves the honours of victory.

I am not pleased with the Senate : I shall not say
a word about political affairs. My only hope is the
confidence I have in that Providence of the Revolution which has accomplished so many miracles. It
continues to rain gold ; the addresses are superb.
Servan, the minister, keeps steadily on. He has
proposed a federation for the 14th of July, which,
by collecting together in Paris an imposing mass of
people from all the departments, might once more
foil that perpetual plot whose threads are retied as
fast as they are broken. I think this is an excellent
idea ; it was enthusiastically received by the majority
and the public. The name of La Fayette is lauded to
the skies ; it is a talisman ; it has a magical effect
that almost looks like sorcery. Chabot, by throwing

a stain on that name, after they had heard fifty denunciations, lost the favour of the Assembly in a moment. Dubayet shouted in a stentorian voice, " They want to disorganize the army; they want to upset France. They want . . . . The hero of the two worlds, the most generous supporter of French liberty," &c.; and all our . . . . applauded, and required that the Assembly should pass a decree consigning to contempt the sacrilegious paper which had spoken of this new god as a man. The fate of France is once more in the hands of La Fayette : We shall see whether he will maintain himself at the height to which he has been raised.

Nothing new from the frontiers, and we are at the end of May. The stagnation, the inaction of our troops, when compared with the natural impetuosity of the French character, is a source of alarm to those who look out ahead.

The porters (*forts*) of the Halles, who call themselves the *forts de la Patrie,* have laid 800 francs on the altar in the Senate House. They demand that the Rights of Man and the Constitution shall be carried at the head of the troops, like the sacred ark, and they were sure that their brothers in arms, fired at the sight as they had been, would force the hand of victory, and vanquish the universe. Petitions and discourses arrive from Athens, Rome, and Sparta. This astonishes many people.

The federation has been decreed. If, unfortunately, you should not be here before the month of

H

July—but I hope you will—I entreat you to be
here for the 14th, with my brother Henry. Last
Monday I heard a splendid military band play the
prophetic air *Ça ira* in the vast hall of the Senate,
and the troops of the line, mingled with the citizens
and the National Guards, repeated the scene that I
have already described to you in a preceding letter.

XXX.

PARIS, *June* 8, 1792.

Let your observations, my dear child, and your
study of men, serve, I entreat you, for your own
advancement in the way of perfection; do not let
the painful spectacle of their defects inspire you
with a guilty self-indulgence and a dangerous inclination to little faults. " Small precautions are the
safeguards of great virtues," says our friend J. J.
Rousseau, with great justice. There are some strong
and privileged souls that walk without swerving in
the path of virtue. If their number be small their
example is great, and you must follow it resolutely.
That is all the preaching you shall have to-day, my
son; I am sparing of it. The quality of the seed,
not the quantity, is what produces an abundant
harvest in good ground.

I hardly dare write about politics to you, lest my
letters should be intercepted. After all, I do not
write them that they may stay on the road; and
from the remarks of Saint-Cyr, and the apprehensions

he has inspired me with as to the fate of my patriotic epistles, I shall write no more of that sort till you have told me whether you receive them safely.

William Priestley presented himself to-day at the National Assembly. He made a very eloquent speech, and had a flattering reception. M. François, who delivered an eulogium of the virtuous Joseph Priestley, was quite equal to the subject. He ranged side by side all those virtues which do honour to philosophy and humanity, and thus composed a touching portrait of the doctor. I recognized it, for I had seen his fine mind in that letter of which I have spoken to you with so much emotion. If you see this venerable man, my son, remember the tender respect your mother bears to him. When I meditate in private on the happiness of yet seeing the earth adorned with great virtues, I think of the doctor, and I hold you fortunate to be enabled to see him in the flesh. Tell me, I beg you, everything you hear about him. The fairest spectacle, to my thinking, is that of great virtue. I could kiss the hem of the philanthropic doctor's garment with the deepest veneration. The National Assembly, wishing to testify their esteem for Dr. Priestley, have decreed that letters of · naturalization shall be granted to his son, William Priestley. They look upon him as the adopted child of the French nation. This is M. François' motion, and doubtless it will pass, for it has been sanctioned already beforehand by public opinion, and was received with applause. It has been sent, for form's sake, to the committee of legislation, that they may make their report with the least possible delay.

I am pleased to hear of the reception you have met with, and curious to get your first letter, which will contain the details of your visit to Lord Stanhope. We French ladies were rather surprised at the terseness of his note, "*I dine at home on Wednesdays*," but our Anglo-French friends assure us that it is a frank and cordial invitation. Messieurs Crouset and Cronier send their love to you, and advise you to penetrate the English bark, which is hard and rough, like that of trees that are formed of the finest wood. As for me, I leave you to your own judgment, and advise you to be prudent. You are not young, because you have learned to think at an early age. Your father has often told me—and you know he is my oracle—that his Jules, left to himself, would never make a false step, because the elevation of his mind and the habit of reflection would keep him straight in every path that leads to good. Your father loves you tenderly; he esteems you, and says a thousand touching and charming things about you to me. He will be fond of *Il Signor Boselini:* make haste to learn Italian; it is the language of tenderness. Your father and I at one time delighted in it; but I am so stupid that I have only remembered enough to be able to read Metastasio with your brother, and to say to you, "*Mio tesoro, mio amico.*" Do you know

I could tell you I love you in nearly every language
if you asked me to do so—but only that—for I was
never good at learning much.

Paris is as still as a lake.

XXXI.

To her Husband.

Paris, *June* 14, 1792.

Last Tuesday I received, at the same time, two
long letters from my two most precious friends.
Yours was opened, and read over and over again
before I touched the other. This involuntary movement of my heart will reveal to you the place you
hold in my affections. I only thought of it myself
after I had steeped my soul in the tenderness of
which both letters are full. And yet, I love my son
with that ardent love which Nature puts into the
maternal heart so abundantly that it seems a
prodigy, and which in my case is carried to its
extreme by two natural causes—my own excessive
sensibility, and the personal merits of our dear
child. After that you will understand that there is
no expression of tenderness that does not seem
weak to me. I feel as if the involuntary proof I
gave when I received your two letters revealed all
the strength of my feelings, but only J. J. Rousseau
could really put such a sentiment into words. As
for me, I consider myself so unworthy of the task

that I stop short at the simple fact, and leave you
to enjoy it.

I have before my eyes six of Jules' letters, which
would make a charming little volume; two to Euvy,
two to Saint-Cyr, and my own two.   I gather
from them a number of most interesting details
on many subjects, but they are, as he says himself,
given at a glance.   The gloomy temperament of
the English people augments his natural disposition to melancholy; and royal despotism, which in
England exercises all its tyranny under the name
of liberty, grieves him almost to the point of
despair.   All he said on that subject to M. Euvy
appeared to me candid and just.   Our Revolution
is not liked in London in general.   The court
detests it, and the people are jealous of it, while
the selfish party in the nation is afraid of its
epidemic effects.   Enlightened philosophy alone
regards it with admiration.   The neutrality that
has been secured is a small political miracle per-
formed by a sacred league.   The rest is intrigue
and corruption, as everywhere else.   Lord Stanhope
looks at Jules from the same point of view from
which you formerly regarded the Abbé Mably.   He
has given him some hints, and it is only by exercising the greatest prudence that our young patriot
is safe in England.   He never goes to the club,
and the French *cafés* are full of government spies,
so that the prudent keep silence.   His letters to
Saint-Cyr breathe the sweetness of his nature, and

are full of descriptions of the novel beauties that Nature offers to his gaze. The sea seems to lend his thoughts the same vast extent that it spreads before his eyes. He clothes everything with fancies that indicate brilliant imagination and profound sensibility. His style is, however, negligent and un-equal, like mine; after something graceful comes a common sentence, brambles with the flowers; but also a facility that can write five pages without taking his pen off. Having first read your letter with delight, I then read it with reflection. I do not think it is without design that you fix my eyes on that peaceful cottage which maintains its tranquillity in the midst of political storms. That ark of the poor will perhaps float in the universal deluge, and virtue will come out of it when the earth has been purified. My soul has flown thither; I was already enjoying by anticipation the happiness of living there with you, when I said to Marion, "Let us go to Dauphiné, in the country we shall be under a less stormy sky than here." Molière was right to consult his servants; mine replied with admirable philosophy, "Madame, we shall no sooner be settled there, than Monsieur will want to make a journey to Paris to look into the state of public affairs." This seemed so probable and natural to me that it is my only answer to that part of your delightful letter. My dear and kind husband, the question to be discussed is whether this plan would not merely vary my troubles and double my anxieties; for I should have to leave Auguste; and his love for me, like mine for him, increases every day, and renders us inseparable until terrible necessity shall impose its irresistible yoke upon us. Tell me if it was the play of your imagination, or an impulse of wisdom which made you wield the pencil of Gesner so artistically; for my mind is still in uncertainty, and that alone would justify in my own eyes the light yet decided manner in which I answer you. Speak to me without figures of speech if you want any more explanations; above all, answer Marion's alarming argument. All this fills my mind with inexpressible agitation. I weep over these absences, which threaten to last my whole life and that of my son, for he, before he left me, gave me the ideas that you ingeniously reproduce in the discourse you put into my mouth. If I had Rousseau's suspicious imagination, Virginie's last letter would appear to me a concerted plan; but I blow upon the bubble, and wait for plainer speech from you, that I may answer by graver reasons. Let us pass to another subject: Yesterday, Boyer brought me the first four numbers of Robespierre's paper.[2] I am sorry I cannot read them with you. They exhibit a really strong and virtuous mind, and set forth truths which strike one's common sense. There is human weakness in them, and the style in general is loose and careless; but there are touches which one finds

[2] *Le Défenseur de la Constitution.*

only when the mind is truly great and pure. Our petty intriguers could not do as much, though they are not wanting in ability. Condorcet, Brissot, Gaudet, and others are, by the very facts, accused before the upright tribunal of reason. All this makes the most intrepid tremble. Robespierre is a man who has devoted himself to the common weal as ardently as the greatest men of antiquity. I am sorry to have to read all this without my best friend, and the light that he can shed on all he deals with. My judgment, obliged to depend on itself, is not halting about Robespierre. He is a Roman exposed to every shaft, and struggling victoriously with and against them all. Pétion, obliged by a combination of circumstances to make a philo-sophical regulation for the decoration of the city and the processions of the Blessed Sacrament, has been reviled by the weak for having professed free principles, and not having the outsides of houses decorated, because on that point individual liberty had been constitutionally established. In short, his enemies employ the blackest and most cunning malice to render him unpopular. The National Guard followed the God of Peace in arms, in disobedience to the municipality. But God, to make everybody of one mind, sent a deluge of rain on the Sunday and the Thursday. The priests, however, who brave Heaven while they pretend to honour it, walked intrepidly along, and, soaked with rain, they dragged the Blessed Sacrament through all the mud of the capital, for it is dragging divinity through the mud when they make it serve the cause of the meanest human passions.

Nothing happened, however, and to-day will pass like Sunday and Thursday. A protecting Providence stretches forth its powerful hand over the poor people, who are duped in every way. Another pip of the apple of discord has caused fresh horrors to spring up. Servan has been denounced by a wretched aristocrat, who has demanded a decree of accusation against him, for having voted the salutary federation that may save Paris from the scourge of civil war if the departments second us, as I have no doubt they will. The corrupt staff has got up a cringing petition, and have exhorted signatures to it by every cowardly means. It was presented to the National Assembly, but the patriots gained the day.

The petition has been treated with the contempt it deserved, and as those who presented it were admitted to the honours of the bar, the indignant Assembly closed the sitting. This cunning act has been condemned by the sections with firmness and eloquence, and protestations against it come in on every side. M. Servan has acquired a great reputation for patriotism. Robespierre calls him a " New Phenomenon :" doubtless, it is the first time a nation rose at the voice of a minister, for Servan said in so many words : " Let the entire nation rise," &c., &c. I myself heard his speech which he delivered in the forcible accents of truth. He has made himself numberless friends and enemies.

On the day of the disbanding of the King's Guards, I read your speech in the electoral assembly at Valence with enthusiasm. This prophet who speaks so well one day would speak equally well on another. Circumstances make men.

Our Assembly does not want intelligence and probity, but it does want an individual of great character, a high-minded man whose noble passion would be the general good, and who would have the strength to act because he would be always borne on the wings of public opinion, whence everything good comes. Our worthy deputies want nothing but a rallying-point; virtue, however, should be united to talent. Chabot, Merlin, and Bazire are mock Mirabeaus; it is said they are zealous patriots : but what men !

Let us embrace, my excellent husband; our principles are the same, the love of virtue and honour inspires us both; my folly is perhaps my wisdom, and . . . . I dare not say it out of respect for you.

Good-bye, I thought to write you a longer letter, but it is easier to send you the evening paper which fills me with indignation against the court, which indignation will perhaps be shared and felt in a manner that will produce an explosion. We are between life and death, through the truly royal malice of all our enemies.

XXXII.

Paris, *June* 16, 1792.

Boyer has brought me the first four numbers of Robespierre's paper. Robespierre is a true Roman; you know how he writes, always with the same principles and the same force, but I think his style is often careless. I look upon him and Pétion as the most virtuous men whom the Revolution has brought forward in spite of their enemies.

Your last letter pained me; you repeat twice, " *I don't know what to fill my paper with,*" and you do not say one word in answer to all my tenderness. You do not smile at the dream inspired by my maternal love, and related, I think, with much warmth of feeling; you do not try to dispel the painful impression it made upon me by the least word. Answer, my son, you whose sensibility is so keen; can the communion between two souls be exhausted? are political events, amusing anecdotes, and original narratives necessary to feed feeling hearts? I am naturally prompt to suppose that there are never effects without causes, and I am now painfully endeavouring to find out whence comes this exhaustion of interest at the commencement of a correspondence that affection should render easy and diffuse rather than cold and constrained. I have said to myself, sadly, perhaps my dear Jules is unhappy, and secretly accuses his mother of cruelly hurrying on our separation. My son, I made you the arbiter of your fate; I took counsel, indeed, and inclined towards the present decision because I thought it a good one. If the measures of prudence which made me consider your instruction, your interest, and happiness, in this journey, have not fulfilled our views; if your stay in London is unpleasant to you; if the study of men you were to make there disheartens you, if the influence of the English character only increases your natural tendency to melancholy—an inclination that I would rather see lessened than encouraged—utter those three words which dilate the soul, "*I am free.*" Consult your reason, sound your inclinations, and carry out with moderation and prudence the resolution which you will have carefully formed. Our arms and our hearts are always open to you. The parental tyranny that cannot endure a change of purpose is far from our thoughts. Wisdom and happiness must be sought for in every way, and one may retrace one's steps without shame. At your age one must examine one's ground, try all roads, until one has found the one in which one can walk with the most useful and satisfactory results. If events are the masters of fools, thoughtful experience is the guide of the wise. Be on your guard against the first impulse of your headstrong impetuosity; subject yourself to the rule of your conscience and your heart.

I am filled with admiration of Lord Stanhope. All you tell me of that great man proves to me that he is after your own heart. His manner of receiving you reminds me of the reception Mably gave your father, when he arrived at Paris with the same purpose as that which has taken you to London—to seek for instruction and knowledge. At the first glance the worthy Abbé Mably was drawn towards him. Twenty years of intimate acquaintance strengthened their mutual esteem, and made us so dear to the kind-hearted philosopher, that we saw him very often; and I, unworthy as I am, passed many a long evening with him, little Jules seated near me, and your brother in my arms. He used to caress you very kindly, and thought I did right to devote myself entirely to my children. There was a superficial coldness about him that gave him an air of great dignity. Try to cultivate Lord Stanhope's friendship; it is among such men as he that you should study nature and seek for your models. I understand Dr. Priestley to be such another man, and I wish you had already seen him. There is still virtue in the world, and the veneration with which it is everywhere regarded proves its value in all eyes and for all hearts. The news from London troubles me sometimes. I earnestly implore you to avoid compromising yourself. Do not be anxious about Paris. Four years of miracles worked by Providence, which thus marks its majestic protection of the people, should make even the incredulous believe.

The king has just changed part of the ministry;

you will see that in the papers. Such daring be-
wilders me; but we shall profit by it, as by all the
rest of his foolish deeds. M. Servan, whom he
breaks like a glass, was really a patriot firm as a
Roman, and capable of the highest views. We
know him personally, and that places my judgment
of him on a solid basis. He had left Romans to
come and take the helm of the war. M. Dumouriez
is in his place; God grant he may be as incorruptible as his predecessor! Gouvion is dead. The
French foolishly exaggerate the loss of officers. It
would seem as if Nature had a special mould for the
ci-devants, and that they alone have any military
talent. Why, Chevert had been a soldier before
he became a general; and there are probably many
young fellows in the army who might become
Turennes but for our foolish prejudices. Just now
uprightness and civic spirit are the most desirable
qualities in our generals, and the most important for
the prosperity of the realm. La Fayette is lauded
to the skies: Luckner agrees with him very well.
Triumphs are expected. I count more on. . . . but
stop, I have been so far from sharing the wild
enthusiasm that turns every head in the crowd, that
I ought modestly to impose on myself the law of
silence. All that I can tell you, for our mutual
benefit, is that true virtue is simple and requires no
ornaments but herself; the luxury which is forced
on virtue by the multitude is unworthy of her real
majesty. Dumouriez is in disfavour. The way in

which he has spoken of his predecessor, and
some sharp remarks on a speech of his at the
Assembly, led to its being thought that he was
won over. The ministers named in the place of
Rolland, Servan, and Clavière are very dubious. It
was announced yesterday in several journals that
Duranton had resigned, being unable to agree with
the Council of anti-revolutionists with which the king
has imprudently surrounded himself. Everything
seems to predict a storm. The king behaves with
such duplicity and bad faith that he inspires honest
people with horror. He stakes his throne and
twenty-five millions of men with as much levity as
he would go a-hunting.

Here is a new event which makes one shudder.
An aristocrat deputy, after vainly provoking Grangeneuve, attacked him in the corridors of the Assembly.
Grangeneuve was wounded, but not dangerously
hurt. The Senate assembled last night to discuss
this terrible affair. Signal justice must be done to
calm the public indignation. The traitor's name is
Jouneau : he is only known by his crime. We are
in a crisis, and I cannot contemplate the result without alarm.

Read attentively in the *Moniteur* Rolland's letter
to the king. It has led to his disgrace at court, and
will win for him the admiration and esteem of all
France. This blindness of kings is the scourge of
humanity ! Truth cannot get near them, and the
fools think that because they reject truth they an-

nihilate it, whereas they only give it additional lustre. Rolland is immortalized.

Do not be anxious about us, my dear child. Do not believe all the lies in the newspapers; but believe in an ever-vigilant and benevolent Providence which will contrive some fresh prodigy to save the country from the barbarous hands that are rending it as-sunder. These events remind me of that line of Racine's—

> " De la chute des rois, funeste avant-coureur."

and these others—

> " Celui qui met un frein au fureur des flots,
> Sait aussi des méchants arrêter les complots."

XXXIII.

To her Husband.

Paris, *June* 19, 1792.

We went to the Maison Commune, where we saw the virtuous Pétion and heard him interrogate the chief of the National Guards about the little aristocrat tricks which had led to his being called before the municipal bar. Everything was gone into; I admired the moderation of the magistrate, and the cunning of the soldier, who alleged that the personal service of each citizen, which has just been ordained by the National Assembly, would be an effectual remedy for the case of which complaint had been made. In short, that you may be aware of every-thing, I must forewarn you to bring your legal exemptions, or you will have to submit to carry the musket in your turn, which would cause me great anxiety because of your sciatica.

The tree of liberty is planted at the door of every *corps de garde,* with joy and patriotism which re-kindle the civic flame. To-morrow it will be planted at the Tuileries itself. The minister has been changed twice since M. Servan's dismissal. The department has refuted Rolland's superb letter. La Fayette addressed one to the Assembly yesterday which it is thought he did not write, the tone is so despotic. He denounces the Jacobin factions, and demands the dispersion of all the clubs. It is feared the royal *veto* will be put upon the decree of the federation. The staff was denounced by the sections, who, in consideration of the public danger, have asked for permanence. Consider all these events taken together, and define in your wisdom what is the catastrophe which is approaching.

To-morrow the people will rise; they will march to the National Assembly, and demand strong measures. The addresses of the sections, which are full of good sense and fairness, have already appeared; that of to-morrow, of which I have had a foretaste from what I heard said at the Commune by an enlightened citizen, will perhaps induce me to go to the National Assembly. I regret your absence; and I feel that if you were here, on the shore of this stormy sea, you would be singularly interested in the flux and reflux of its waves, and in spite of your philosophy and love of repose, you would be better than where you are.

Dusault does wonders. The Assembly falls and rises again. We shall see what attitude it will assume in the chaos of events which make the most courageous tremble. A Mirabeau would bend his brows like Jupiter, and all would go well; but he is in his grave.

They say the King of Hungary is dead, the city of Berlin in insurrection, and all Brabant ready to raise the sacred standard of liberty. The Prussian ministry has fallen; we must wait for the confirmation of all this; but some of it may be true, for the echoes repeat it on every side.

The decree concerning the priests and that for the assembling of 20,000 men are vetoed. The fifth No. of Robespierre's paper condemned that measure, for reasons which appear good, but are diametrically opposed to those that procured it the honour of the *veto*. The *Révolution de Paris* traces the source of our troubles to the constitution itself, by the strange prerogatives it accords to the royal individual who is all-powerful to do evil. It says that only the frontal of the edifice can be preserved, while Robespierre asserts that not the smallest stone must be touched for fear it should fall altogether. This conflict of opinions is distressing. The last four numbers of the *Révolution de Paris* inspire me with dread and distrust. The people wanted to go to-day, armed as in '89, from the National Assembly to the palace of the Tuileries to present their petitions. The department, with its aristocratic prudence, promptly passed a resolution against the assembling of all armed crowds, charging the municipality to take the necessary measures to prevent it, and rendering the Mayor of Paris responsible for the public safety. Poor Pétion! Poor Pétion! What pain it is for your friends, who see you between Scylla and Charybdis. May Heaven protect him! He is virtue itself; but the processions have made the people hostile to his philosophy, and it was the department that had cunningly forced him to proclaim it openly. What intrigues and tricks!

Marion went into the Tuileries Gardens yesterday evening. There were more people than grains of sand, all talking in the same way. They demand that the king shall either loyally support the constitution, or be its declared enemy. They demand plain dealing, and loyalty *à la Française.* This will lead to the *dénouement* of a tragedy that is keeping all minds in a mortal anguish, worse than death.

La Fayette's pretended letter was laid on the desk by an invisible hand; and it is now known to be false; but what a mean artifice!

Wednesday evening, 20th.
(Anniversary of the Oath of the *Jeu de Paume.*)

What a grand day! What a triumph! What

signal protection is extended by Heaven to the good people. I started at about eleven o'clock; and in crossing the Place du Carrousel I saw a triple row of cavalry ranged along the walls and doors of the palace, the whole length of that vast enclosure. An immense crowd of curious people filled the remaining space, and extended as far as the National Assembly. I made my way at last to the stairs of your gallery.

M. Duverbray assured me it was filled, so I went to M. Euvy's, and got a place between Mdlles. Canot and Julliot, with Auguste by my side. Poor Marion was outside, and remained at the Tuileries till seven o'clock. By this means you will know all that passed both inside and out, for Marion has the eye and ear of a philosophic observer.

The Assembly had never appeared more majestic and brilliant, not one empty place; four or five thousand people in the different parts, in profound silence, or violent agitation, according to the matter in hand.

The department arrived at the bar; La Rochefoucauld, Demennier, &c. Rœderer was the speaker. He said that gatherings were forbidden by the constitution, that the one which was advancing had been interdicted by a resolution of the directory, that he was sure the mass of the people was pure, but that the malevolent, &c. The wisdom of the Assembly would know what measures to take, and the galleries, sullen and moody, glance

with indignation at this constituted authority,
which crosses the hall under the disapproving
silence with which you are acquainted. Vergniaud goes up to the tribune ; every heart follows
him. He sets forth with moderation the reasons
why the people should be received, although by
the terms of the constitution they are in the wrong.
He touches no loud chords ; they are not necessary
for persuasion. In the Constituent Assembly and
in this one, the envoys of the different sections or
battalions have been received. What motive can
they then assign to these envoys for an unjust and
cruel refusal ? The number of armed citizens was
about 30,000. The infamous Dumolard ascended
the tribune with all the rage of a Catiline. After
having invoked the Constitution, he said that all the
rigour of the law must be exerted to prevent the
admission of this multitude. Ramon had the daring
to speak in the same way, but with less vehemence.
Paris would have been deluged with blood if Dumolard had been listened to. The fury of the minority,
and the indignation of the majority, produced a
tumult that obliged the President to put on his hat.
Vergniaud returned to the tribune, he repeated what
he had already said, and redoubled the admiration
and the hopes of those who listened to him in the
deepest silence. Gaudet spoke in his turn, and on
the subject of the department he uttered the following little epigram: "A Roman emperor who wanted
to catch the people infringing the law, had it written

in such an ambiguous way that the poor people were always guilty!" The department had its resolution of yesterday posted up on the walls to-day, when our thirty thousand men were in motion. You must know that the people had not taken this step without informing the department, through the municipality. The horrible catastrophe of the Champ de Mars was called to mind; it would be the same over again! This remembrance struck terror to all hearts. At last, after several little incidents, the great majority decreed the admission of the petitioners to the bar. La Source said there was also a petition for the king, that he would lay it, if the Assembly wished, on the bureau, so that they might make such use of it as their wisdom should dictate. Immediately a motion was made to send a deputation of sixty members to the château of the Tuileries. This measure, which was not decreed, was instantly executed by the "blacks," who went out in a rage, and I have since heard that they remained with the king all the rest of the day.

The petitioners being at the bar, an orator, a second Cicero, spoke with such eloquence that he carried conviction to every mind, setting forth sublime ideas and simple truths with such persuasive sentiment, and such irresistible logic, that one would have wished to be all ears, that one might the better hear him. The general admiration secured silence, which was as profound and majestic as the speech itself. On concluding, the speaker was greeted with applause and bravos that made the roof of the Senate ring. François, who presided, answered coldly and stupidly, as he has done everything else. Then came the printing of the petition, honourable mention, the honours of the sitting for the petitioners. Right of access to the Assembly for all citizens were decreed by acclamation. All the people were afoot; the true sovereign displayed true majesty; two hours by the watch had passed in perfect order, in magnificent tranquillity. There were to be seen citizens armed with pikes, National Guards, chasseurs, grenadiers, troops of the line, ladies, women of the people—all mingled together in the true spirit of equality and fraternal union. The sacred tables of the Rights of Man, and a number of emblems of the constitution and of liberty, were carried by the people. A military band played *Ça ira.* The two faubourgs, Saint Antoine and Saint Marceau, were united, and this was shown by an allegorical picture with the device, *L'Union fait la force.* They were 40,000 strong. The uniformity of this new procession was broken by frequent changes of the objects which it presented to the eye, and this kept one's attention alive. It was also interrupted by several pleasant incidents. The banners had got twisted together in saluting the President, and shouts were raised for union. An individual, dressed like a rustic, suspended its progress for a moment, to say a few sensible and forcible words upon the war. M. Santerre, who came at the end, gave a superb banner in the name of the faubourgs. The President stopped the last group in the hall, to inform the people and the Assembly at the same time that the brave Luckner had taken Courtrai, that he had made more than a thousand prisoners of war; and that the German inhabitants of the city had shouted, "Long live *the French nation.*" La Fayette is strongly suspected of having written the letter; all his sentiments are to be recognized in it; he is half-unmasked. Let us wait, let us wait.

Marion has seen surprising things. The people went into the king's house, and presented two cockades to him—one tri-colour, the other white. Louis took the three colours, and put on the red cap. Superb things were said to him; no doubt the petition was given to him. All these details must wait until to-morrow, if I can then collect them with certainty. Marion was at the Tuileries with 200,000 souls; she saw the people at all the windows of the château, making signs of peace and satisfaction. They say the king's wife went away in the morning; I do not know whither.

Thursday Morning.

The night has passed quietly. The hairdresser, who has already spread the morning's news throughout the house, assures us that the people have everywhere displayed the utmost moderation and good sense. They were directed by intelligent and enlightened leaders. My *fidus Achates* had observed yesterday that all these movements were regulated and measured. The people succeeded in getting the door of the château opened to them, as much by the strength of their reasoning, as by the force of their numbers, and it was said on every side, "The people will do nothing unworthy of them; they desire only justice and loyalty." The aristocrats, who had hoped to turn this event into the beginning of a civil war, spread innumerable false rumours throughout Paris. It was said that the château had been pillaged, and a thousand other calumnies were circulated. The false brethren in the National Guard, the Fayettists, were at bay. Twice they shut the gates of the garden, and twice they were made to open them. It was remarked that there were three or four officers in each patrol, and a cordon of epaulets all along the terrace on the edge of the water. The great majority kept themselves in such perfect union, and behaved with so much reciprocal attention, that not the smallest accident occurred. The people pressed the king to observe the constitution, and to fulfil his promises. It is said that the brave Pétion went to the château, urged the people to withdraw, and answered, with his own life, for the successful issue of the event.

The king is going to-day to the National Assembly. All is quiet; and already, though it is only eight o'clock, there is a great stir and much animation. The queen was with her husband. She gave her son over to M. Santerre, that he might take him in his arms, and show him to the people. I must acknowledge that the reports are so confused, I am unable to attest the truth of what I tell you; but this is certain, that the order of this fair disorder, and the general tranquillity, together with the good French public spirit, have made a real civic festival of the event. I have never seen so much suavity and open-hearted gaiety, mingled at the same time with a certain pride, and with dignity which rendered laughter imposing.

There was a terrific crowd on the Pont Neuf, when I crossed it at about six o'clock. They were planting a tree of liberty. The *Samaritaine* rang out *Ça ira* with its *carillon.* Henri Quatre seemed to beat time to the music, such was the influence of patriotism over men and the elements. Oh, why are you not here? I should then see through your eyes; for I would much rather stay at home; but the desire to see, so that I may give an account to you, and my love of the people, founded upon the true love of justice and humanity, fill me with such urgent solicitude that I cannot remain inactive, when I feel that they are in danger. My curiosity is that of the heart. Yesterday I had an attack of fever, because I was for a while uncertain of their fate.

This day is full of interest. Cowardice is the characteristic of the Senate. To be great it must be elevated by the people. What will be said and done then? The king is going thither. The

40,000 citizens entered, as usual, by the gate opposite the Place Vendôme, and came out by the long
narrow court of the Riding-School. They defiled on
the terrace before the château, which they completely surrounded, and entered the building by the
doors of the Place du Carrousel. I observe to-
day, on cool reflection, that Vergniaud and Gaudet
did not utter any of those things which proceed
from great minds on a great occasion. Their
strongest argument was, that since the people had
been received they must receive the king. A strong
mind would have found and assigned many other
arguments. But the petition has said everything.
I am assured that the king drank to the health of
the nation from the necks of several bottles of wine,
which he then presented to the officers.

He had asked for time to reflect upon the two
vetos, until ten o'clock this morning. Imagine the
shrieks of our toads of ' blacks ' over the restric-
tion of the royal liberty, but since he uses it only to
do evil, the fetters of the king make the freedom of
the people.

XXXIV.

Paris, *June* 23, 1792.

Take care of your health, write to us frequently,
and guard yourself against the gloom of the English
temper. If I had known it better, I should not
have been so ready to send you to study men in a
country where Nature seems to have created them

in a fit of melancholy. If, however, the sombre
aspect which England presents to you be sufficiently disagreeable to your eyes to drive the
subject which sometimes masters you from your
thoughts, you may turn the correctness of all your
observations into a wholesome remedy. When one
has been endowed by Heaven with an upright heart
and sound intelligence, when one has friends to
love, and one's fellow to serve, existence is so
sweet, that at each step in life one ought to thank
the Supreme Being for having given it, and far
from scattering thorns upon one's own path, one
ought to try to avoid them, and to gather flowers by
the wayside. Health of mind and body makes all
Nature smile upon us. How great are her charms
for the feeling-hearted, how many the enjoyments
she affords to the pure-minded ! My dear boy, what
advantages we possess over the vulgar, in the
delightful sensations with which we are inspired by
the natural beauty of the fields, the murmuring
streams, a fair prospect, and the deep shade of the
woods. How can any one be unhappy, who is so
organized as to feel vividly the charm of beautiful
Nature, and that of virtue still more powerful ?

True happiness consists in knowing one's self
thoroughly; because then one undertakes nothing
that is beyond one's strength, and, carefully exa-
mining one's ground, makes no false steps. The
phantoms of the imagination, which ought always to
be blown away by the breath of reason, are the

chief origin of your melancholy dreams. I beg of
you to let those which concern your papa and
myself be all rose-colour. We love you as our son
and our friend; we desire for you wisdom and
happiness. Prejudices and the follies of fortune are
nothing to us; but the wish of my maternal heart
is that you should extract content from the various
situations in which the caprices of fate may place you.

This is all that you shall have from me to-day.
What a description I might have given you of the
triumph of the people, and their majestic tranquillity
in the proud attitude that they assumed yesterday!
What a spectacle for an observer, friendly to mankind, and how attractive is the mingling in the
French character of sublime greatness with all the
charm of gaiety! It makes a civic festival of what
is a terrible catastrophe in appearance, and Paris
was never more calm and joyous than in the midst
of this strange agitation of a great people. I have
seen and heard everything. I went yesterday to
the National Assembly, and through the streets, and
into the public places, and I assure you I could find
nothing to observe, except proofs of the goodwill
and generosity of a great multitude assembled
under the banner of fraternity. The petition was
worthy of Demosthenes.

Rest assured, my son, that France has faced
round, and that she will be free, in spite of the little
men who are opposing her. At their head I place,
to my great regret, several of our chief political

leaders who break on the morrow their promises of the day before. I found my judgment on three general observations: the shower of gold which falls continuously for the expenses of the war; the trees of liberty which are being planted at the gates of all the *corps de garde* of our capital, in every corner of the realm, and which will soon cover the surface of the country; and the lofty and sublime sentiments breathed in every petition.

My desire to give vent to my thoughts on this great subject is suddenly arrested by the fact, always present with me, that if I yield to it my letters may not reach you. I am afraid to give you opinions the holding of which is prohibited where you are.

I was present to-day at the sitting of the National Assembly. In the gallery with me was a remarkably clever woman, an intimate friend of M. and Madame Pétion. She gave me circumstantial details of the communications which took place yesterday between the people's magistrate and the executive power. The man-king does not play the *beau rôle* in them. But she also gave me a delightful account of our brave Pétion and his wife in their private life. In that moral interior virtue dwells, my son; only the good man can be a hero in his dressing-gown, and all that this woman, who has known Pétion for twenty years, told me about him, redoubles my esteem and admiration.[3]

---

[3] Two years and six months after this letter was written, the youth of seventeen, to whom it was addressed, was in prison

I also saw a great lady, a friend of the Orleans family, who assured me that the father and the sons are all in the army, as quiet and as safe as the simplest citizens. The stories told about them are merely pitiful insults to reason.

I am glad to tell you, by-the-bye, that the *Moniteur* is often untrustworthy. This I have observed with my own eyes on important occasions. It favours Dumolard: in that you have its secret. It slides over a circumstance in which he displayed all the beauties of character of the despicable Roman Catiline. My free speaking will out, you see. Tell me, my dear son, if this is *inconvenient.* I like that new word. But to return.

I shall always lecture you on the necessity for guarding against your imagination, which is a very microscope. Tell me whether you have seen the worthy Dr. Priestley, and whether you see much of Lord Stanhope. We are very quiet in Paris; do not believe any bad political news, unless you hear it from me. I do not "lie like a *Gazette,*" nor do I see everything " *en noir,*" like the timid folk.

XXXV.

PARIS, *June* 24, 1792.

We are all breathless here, such is the rapidity with which event succeeds event, and the storm-

with the wife and son of Pétion. Madame de La Fayette was in the same prison at the same time.

clouds are gathering. Nothing very terrible as yet, however. The affair on Wednesday, which I described to you, will perhaps have unfortunate results because the Assembly is yielding. A decree by which more precise measures against armed assemblies are prescribed, has been issued to-day. The proclamation by the king, made yesterday, has been so profusely posted that there are five between my abode and M. Creusot's. It is so calumnious, and so far removed from the truth, that it excites general indignation. But, unhappily, the bourgeois aristocracy, and the large number of moderates who profess to desire the constitution, maintain that the people ought to remain perfectly quiet because the laws will set everything right. A proclamation by the municipality is in the same sense, and if, to-morrow, the poor "people" dares to show itself, as it threatens to do, an end will be made of it. To-morrow will be an ominous day. I am in hopes that the leaders of the people will take the fatal combination of the constituted authorities into consideration, and save them from so great a danger, and therefore I do not think there will be any popular movement to-morrow, in spite of the machinations of all those who desire that such a movement should take place, for it would open our gates to civil war.

Our affairs are in a worse state than I have ever seen them in, on account of the folly of certain people who pretend that the constitution is violated

by the people, just as if the king had respected its
virginity! The poor Jacobins are charged with
this crime, and they are anathematized on all
sides. I remarked, on Wednesday, that 200,000
people followed the procession of 40,000; if
the Jacobins have excited and urged on all those
they are powerful indeed. Then, another absurdity,
they pay the multitude! The most pitiable nonsense
of this kind is talked, and the differences of opinion
among the patriots is very unfortunate. Nevertheless, in spite of all this, I hope there are a
sufficient number of enlightened men among them
to save the commonwealth.

The king has worn the red cap; crime of the
people! Pétion has spoken to him with the dignity
of a man; crime of the magistrate! It would seem
as though he were still King of France, and not King
of the French, to judge by the way in which his
foolish resentments are humoured. The ministers
appeared at the Assembly yesterday: *a goodly show
of noxious beasts.* Guadet gave them a proper
handling, but there is something brewing in the
Senate. Everything is referred to the Council of
Twelve, to which belong Guiton, who seems strong,
Brissot, Condorcet, and Gensonné, who do not
speak. What is to become of us? Things have
never seemed to me so dark as they look to-day.

M. Bouchy did not fail to speak kindly to me
about the political principles of the Montaigne
Club. I said to him, frankly, that they were

Feuillants. He thinks that the "executive power" is traitorous and perfidious, but that it is the business of the constitution to drive him along. We must wait and see, and above all, we must respect the constitution; this armed populace is not the true people, it is composed of foreigners, of ruffians, or of what used formerly to be called the dregs of the people; those who having nothing have no interest except in disorder. I said, with as much moderation as possible, all I could say, but to my mind the bourgeois aristocracy, which causes this terrible separation in the popular class, is more dangerous than all. The drum beats everywhere. The battalion of Sainte Geneviève is already afoot.

As I was crossing the Place du Panthéon an officer said to me, "Madame, we are going to support the law;" and he walked away. A soldier replied, "We are not of his opinion. Bah! *Ça ira;* we will not fire."

I told you yesterday it was the proclamation that was posted so profusely; but it is the king's letter in which he demands the assembling of forty-two battalions to form a camp between the capital and the frontiers. This is almost the same demand as that made by M. Servan, which led to his disgrace, and the decree which was vetoed. I cannot understand this royal artifice. He will, and he will not; he places his veto upon a decree of the Corps Législatif, which calls for the assembling of 20,000 men, and then he orders up forty-two battalions.

I am confident that all this fuss about the National
Guard will be nothing more than talk.   If the
people moved, their strength would be so great that
the guard could do nothing.   But their leaders will
not expose them to the danger of the day.   On
Wednesday, Saint-Huvergne was at the head of the
citizens, and Santerre at the head of the soldiers.

On Wednesday, when the mayor went for the last
time to the château, the king said to him angrily,
"Peace, peace! be silent!"   "Sire," replied Pétion,
"the people's magistrate must not suffer silence to
be imposed on him," and he continued to speak.
Fancy the rage of the court with this worthy man.

I sent, this morning, to ask Mademoiselle Chrétion
to come to me.   I had not seen her for a month.
She assures me that the people, who are in very
wise hands, will not stir; that their last great
gathering was conducted so ably, that, among
the whole 40,000, there were no individuals who
were not guaranteed, either by the various patriotic
societies, or by the sections; and in the case
of soldiers, by the battalions.   An irresistible
argument to be opposed to the rumours of calumny
is that Louis XVI., his wife, his children, and his
court, are alive and perfectly well; and that no
sentiments were expressed towards them but such
as ought to have awakened remorse in them, and
would have touched hearts susceptible of any
generosity.

The king took the red cap and put it on his head

of his own accord; his portrait has been taken already. This prince, whose weakness leads him into falsehood and perfidy, proudly adorned his brow with the symbol of liberty; in his lying recriminations against the people he has trodden it underfoot. His letter to the Assembly, his proclamation, the *procès-verbaux* drawn up because some one struck at his door with a pickaxe, all this reveals the despot, who has a Monk at the head of an army, to punish those insolent persons that dare to regard him as a man.

This morning I went to the Place du Panthéon, on which were three battalions with their guns, and lighted fuses. There were hardly any except officers there. It is a pretty regiment of *plats à barbe,* for that is the nickname for them. The women were making fun of them and their uniform. "These gentlemen," said one, "must surely expect that it is going to rain Austrians, for they are too gallant to kill Frenchmen." Another said, "This is then the army of Coblentz, they have all got epaulets." They stood about there until one o'clock, when they retired. I saw and heard all this with joy. In short, my dear, the storm has been turned aside. Patience and courage! I cannot resist sending you the evening paper, I have read all the interesting matter it contains with so much pleasure.

At seven o'clock in the evening we went to the *ci-devant* College of Navarre, and squeezed ourselves into the gallery of our section. We heard it declared that the Commandant-General and M. Pétion had lost the confidence of the nation. The section of the Lombards announces that they have made up bales of all their National Guard uniforms, to be sent to the regiments of volunteers who are in need of them, and that, henceforth, the dwellers in that section will serve in their ordinary dress. An address to the National Assembly, demanding the reduction of the sixty battalions to forty-eight, the number of the sections, and the suppression of the staff, was voted. All this, and also a motion that the address of the Faubourg Saint Antoine, which you will read in the Journal, should be read to the National Assembly, was received with loud applause.

Bouchy had said to me, "Madame J——, go just once to our section; you will see that it is impossible to hold by it, they are mere mad *sans culottes* there." I am not indeed of their opinion. D——, who was president, sent in his resignation this evening, being of the party of the Feuillantins of the Montaigne Club. The public spirit of the people is perfect; it is only the bourgeois aristocracy which deprives the societies of the support which they would have received from the enlightened portion of the people, but all is not lost; and *Ça ira* in spite of the knaves and the fools.

Marion and I unite in regretting your absence. What a pity M. J—— is not here, how much his great and noble mind would find to enjoy? There are still sudden dangers, in which protecting

Heaven so favours the imposing mass of the true and faithful that the people triumph over all the devices of the artful policy of courts, and the infamous calumnies of their hired scribblers. Every day, addresses, full of the language of truth, are received from the departments. One has come from Dijon which is worthy of Cicero.

XXXVI.

PARIS, *June* 26, 1792.

I advise you to be most prudent and circumspect in the enunciation of your sentiments respecting the French Revolution and the English constitution. Here, the rod of despotism is ever uplifted to repress every kind of liberty. I was far from thinking the case was the same where you are, but all that I observe in the public papers would make me seriously uneasy if I had less confidence in your good sense. I like your Lord Stanhope just as I liked the Abbé Mably. I advise you to cultivate to the utmost so valuable an acquaintance; if he can place you in an English family on the conditions of which we have already spoken, it will be for you, acting on your own experience, to tell us what sum will be required for your maintenance. I am anxious to hear that you have also seen Dr. Priestley. I conclude that these two great men, compatriots and contemporaries, must be friends. I want to know whether you assiduously frequent the philosopher-

lord. Do not fail to·present your mother's respects
to him, and to express the gratitude which he has
awakened in a maternal heart, deeply sensible of
the kind interest which he takes in you and full of
profound veneration for his virtues. You are, however, at liberty to dismiss this motion and return
to the former question if you think proper, for I
cannot divine the *à propos* that there may be in
this, and the *à propos* is a great point. At any rate
present my respects to these great men. And tell
me about Fox, for I esteem him highly. Is he
somewhat of a prophet in his own country ? Relate
to me the use you make of your time, and how
you are getting on with the English language.
Tell me, also, whether you are pursuing other
studies.

Public opinion is taking form upon all the events
which have bewildered the wisest, and, notwithstanding the foolish division among the patriots,
the great majority, enlightened by their good sense,
and guided by strict integrity, approve and sanction
the constitutionally-unconstitutional action of the
people. They have grasped the spirit of the law,
without holding by its letter, like the moderate
Feuillantins, who prefer to perish in due form rather
than be saved by a lucky breach of rule, would have
them to do. Absolute quiet reigns in the capital ;
but, just as in stormy weather, the sun shines out
brightly only to be veiled anew by clouds, which
will again discharge rain, hail, and tempest, so our

tranquillity is only the forerunner of fresh troubles, and this momentary rest, which the exhaustion produced by recent events has rendered necessary, is but the precursor of disturbance. If the " executive power " were well directed the constitution would work satisfactorily, but on the contrary, it seems to toy with its own destruction, and its calumnious recriminations upon the decided action of the poor people are clear indications that if it were but strong enough it would resort to barbarous methods of repression. The multitude are justified, and the purity of their intentions is proved, by the fact that not a hair of any head has been injured in this great movement of an outraged people. The king, his wife, his children, their courtiers, and their wives, have all been respected, and the effervescence of 600,000 people has not produced, thank Heaven ! the slightest crime. The entrance into the Louvre is a very venial sin, and if Titus had been there on that great day in the costume of Louis XVI., he might have deserved the title so dear to human nature, simply by manifesting the most ordinary qualities of an honest man. He took the red cap, and put it on with an appearance of sincere good-will that filled the spectators with delight. The demand that he should rescind his vetoes was made with moderation, some stupid coarse expressions only excepted, and these were uttered, no doubt, by enemies of the people, at the moment when entrance to the den was gained. Nothing disgraceful or low soiled the deeds of so strange and bright a day.

In vain is everything done to corrupt public opinion, the truth shines out, and the National Guard, notwithstanding the wiles of a great number of its officers, is staunch in the main. The patriotic societies, which weed themselves and multiply themselves at the moment when a terrible war is declared against the mother society, shed floods of light abroad, and keep up such incessant vigilance that there is no escape from their indefatigably active perspicuity.

The affair was effected so cleverly, and there was such perfect concert among the different civic corps, that, if they had not entered the Louvre, there would not have been even a peccadillo against the law ; but the number of instruments will sometimes interrupt the harmony of even the best-arranged concert. The true friends of concord in the various parties, see so clearly that the friends of the constitution means peace, that the very persecution which they sustain attaches them to it. There are more Jacobins, to use the established word, than ever.

The departments begin to deliver their sentiments upon the popular movement of the 20th of June, which makes, within one day, the anniversary of the 21st—that memorable date of last year, marked by the shameful flight of the executive power and its cowardly desertion of its post. If it had not been for the sublime calmness of the people, that desertion would have plunged the realm into the fury of civil war. Let us then weigh those two events in the strict balance of justice. The famous protest of the king against the constitution, and the people's love for it, form the test by which to try those who seek to support or to overthrow it. The departments, as I have said, are speaking. The small minority, the organs of calumny, cry shame upon the people, and flatter the court. The imposing majority speaks the proud language of free men, and, to deliver an impartial judgment it is enough to know that two and two make four, and to make an honest reckoning of those who flatter, and those who venture to tell the truth. If the result produced be six to one, the majority is a fifth, and this is the calculation already made and proved by what has appeared. I went yesterday to the National Assembly, and heard addresses read from Lyons, Laval, Brest, Abbeville, and Péronne. I beg you to read all these in the *Moniteur,* if indeed its usual benignity does not make it leave out the most vigorous, on which they "pass to the order of the day," because weak eyes, hurt by the bright light of truth, cannot bear its brilliance, and unite with its enemies to cover it with clouds that hide it from view.

Would you believe that I am inclined to put my veto upon all the bad things you say of our "Anglomanes"? It seems to me, my dear Jules, that you, who are so kind-hearted and have so much philanthropy, ought not to pronounce so severely, after a first glance, on a nation who have been for so long the admired of others, and who hold the first rank in Europe among free and humane peoples. You must forgive me, my dear child, I have a heart which does not permit me to be philosophical, and so much do I love indulgence and kindness that I call upon yours on behalf of your hosts, that they may soften the colours of the picture, even though Nature presents it to you with all the English shadows. I implore you to be always on your guard against your ardent imagination, and against the ideal of mankind which you form for yourself. Learn to know men thoroughly. They are good in general; society has spoiled them a little, although they were made for society. No; we were not made to live in the woods, and go on all fours, as one sometimes wishes to do when one reads your great friend Jean Jacques Rousseau. So, my dear, let us accustom ourselves to look at our fellow-men, at their vices and their virtues, to avoid the former with horror, and to imitate the latter with ardour. Above all, no mask of hypocrisy; that is the greatest deformity of Nature.

Friday Evening.

Little did I think when I wrote my last sentence yesterday, that La Fayette would throw off the mask and reveal the features of a Cromwell. He

appeared at the bar of the National Assembly at the
moment when such a proceeding was least expected.
Yesterday, in the afternoon, he denounced the
" attempt on the Tuileries," speaking with all the
boldness of a Catiline. This scene, which no
doubt was prepared beforehand, produced nothing
except indignation in the galleries; the Assembly
did not manifest any, it seemed to be struck with
amazement. I had an idea that the morrow of so
singular a day would be marked by some great trait
of patriotism; but nothing happened. A calumnious
denunciation against the Jacobins, which produced
no result; then a vague statement by the six
ministers, and a letter from Luckner to the king,
in the same spirit as the fine speech of the other
general—he demands respect for the hereditary
representative, for the chief functionary, the supreme
head of the army;—a proclamation of the same
principles by the king to the army; afterwards, to
mix and season all this, a little victory of La
Fayette's force, adapted to circumstances, just like
a fairy tale; and that was all, except the reference
of everything to the Commission of Twelve.

I am not well satisfied with the Assembly. It
accorded the honours of the sitting to La Fayette,
yesterday, as to a petitioner. He had seated himself in the midst of the aristocrats, but he was
dislodged and conducted to the bench set apart for
the bearers of petitions. They say he went away
this morning, but I do not know. This truly

extraordinary man has made public opinion take backward steps in all the different stages of our Revolution, and, in the name of liberty, serves its enemies. I cannot yet calculate the outcome of his new exploit. He has acknowledged his letter with all the confidence of a man who feels his strength. He had denounced the Jacobins in most despotic fashion. His best friends do not know what to say. Luckner's letter is only an insignificant supplement, and it is attributed to his colleague. It has only slightly injured the confidence that is accorded *to him, Luckner.*

Adieu, my dear boy, we are, and shall be for a long time in a state of agitation; be very prudent and circumspect. If Mirabeau had been at the Assembly yesterday, the general would have remained in the lobby. He knew how to strike great blows with that weapon of the *à propos,* which is always victorious; but men of character and determination, where are they in the Senate? Talent is not sufficient.

Try to be happy, and do not regret Paris at this moment, although it be apparently quiet, for storms are brewing. The apathy of the Senate is the despair of honest people, who feel that it may yet prove our ruin and its own.

XXXVII.

To her Husband.

Paris, *June* 30, 1792.

La Fayette has appeared at the bar of the Assembly to acknowledge his letter boldly, and to denounce the nation in what he calls "the attempt against the king" committed by the people on the 20th June. He had prepared the way for this *coup de théâtre* by the customary machinations of the court, so that the Senate appeared to be petrified, and poor Guadet was the only person who spoke. If a strong and determined man had acted with vigour, and represented this proceeding of the general's in its true light he would not have been admitted. " A general coming to dictate his will to the National Assembly outrages the law ; he shall not enter here except over the corpses of the legislators ! " This single sentence might have saved France from the horrors which are being prepared for her. The galleries, the good patriots, public opinion, all would have thrilled with joy. He was admitted, he spoke, he decried the people, he denounced the Jacobins. Girardin thanked him, and accorded him the honours of the sitting. He placed himself between Dumas and Dumolard ; he was requested to pass on to the petitioners' bench ; and all this passed in the dull silence of despair, notwithstanding the applause on the bad side.

Yesterday it was expected that the Assembly would have revealed itself. I was there. The order of the day was proceeded with, as if nothing had happened, and this after a denunciation of the Jacobins which was proved to be utterly false and malicious. The six ministers came and prosed until every one fell asleep, and their statements were peacefully referred to the Commission of Twelve. The Minister of War read to the Assembly a letter from Luckner to the king, in which he assures the king that all his forces, sharing his sentiments, disapprove of the audacious deed of the people. He said that certain instructions which it was necessary to communicate to the Assembly, but not publicly, were added to this letter. The General Committee was almost demanded; the matter was, however, sent up to the Diplomatic Committee. The minister than read a proclamation to the army in the spirit of La Fayette, and no doubt dictated by him, although made in the name of the king, and signed "Louis." Afterwards, to varnish over all these horrors, a little victory by the hero of liberty was announced; and then they passed to the great order of the day, which was the fixing of the age of marriage. The public murmured loudly. The Assembly is ruining us and itself. The good deputies are in despair; the ministers are fooling them palpably. If the departments do not yield, the constitution will be blown away by cannon, in the name of the constitution and the law: to this pass we have come.

Everything is going ill! The conduct of the Assembly is so irritating to the people, that I am convinced when Louis XVI. shall think proper to take the whip of Louis XIV., wherewith to drive out this feeble parliament, " bravos " will be raised on every side, inspired by very different feelings, it is true, but what do the tyrants care so that the chorus is in their favour? The bourgeois aristocracy is in high delight, the people are cast down, and in despair; thus is the storm brewing.

Ah, why am I not in our cottage with you? The dismissal of the patriotic ministers has been dictated by the general; the new ministers are all of his selection. Bouillé's cousin wants to make of all France a Champ de Mars. You see our misfortune; the partisans of this extraordinary man believe that they offer you an irresistible argument when they say the aristocrats speak of him as you do.

I shall see about coming to a decision, if public affairs continue to afflict us. As we can do nothing in them, we must wrap ourselves in our mantles and bend our head to the axe of despotism. Auguste said, last evening, that I must tell you that we would go and join you, that we would remain in Dauphiné until the month of November, and that in the meantime, either La Fayette will have overthrown the constitution in the name of the constitution, or he will be overthrown himself by a fresh rising, and thus, one way or another, we shall know what

L

to reckon on. There are many tempests shut up within the volcano on which we live.

Pétion has just so many friends as there are pure hearts and just minds.

The directory of the department is of the court party, and draws up despotic acts with great success.

If the Assembly had openly condemned La Fayette's letter, he would not have ventured to appear; if, when he appeared at the bar he had been met with cries of resistance, he would not have dared to read Luckner's letter to the king, which was prompted by La Fayette. It is La Fontaine's fable of the female dog :—

> "Prêtez-moi votre loge pour mettre bas.
> Attendez que mes enfants soient grands ;
> Puis elle montre les dents."

I think, however, that they have made their attempt too soon, and that the union of the people will effect a counterpoise. But the Senate! The Senate! That perfidious revision, sanctioned by the protection of La Fayette, is a sad example of what it can do. If it lent its assistance to a really constitutional king, it would have France for it; but it spread its shield then over a perjured king, taken *in flagrante delicto,* and to-day it enables him to triumph.

Since the *fête* at Château Vieux, we have been going down, though fighting always. I shall go

and join you if La Fayette continues to lead our
deputies in the fatal direction which they seem
disposed to take. He will then select Paris, if he
can, for the theatre of war, and I remember so well
the terror caused by those legal assassinations in the
Field of the Federation, that I would rather not be
here on a similar occasion. As he quits his post *a
capriccio*, if it pleased the people to rise once more,
in their indignation, he might set off for Paris, and
arrive soon enough to inspire the gangrened portion
of the National Guard with the boldness to fire upon
them ; and then our ills would be incalculable.

XXXVIII.

PARIS, *July* 4, 1792.

You know that Ramond said La Fayette was the
eldest son of liberty. Collot d'Herbois, in a discourse delivered at the Jacobins' Club, said : " If
he be the eldest son of liberty, he assassinates his
mother ; if he be our elder brother, he is our Cain !"
All France talks, with Roman earnestness, of the
unconstitutional and criminally despotic proceedings
of the general. In truth, all the springs of eloquence
are refreshed and revived for the French. Cicero,
and Demosthenes live once more among us, in many
persons. Read Vergniaud, in the *Moniteur;* there
is not a private petition that does not reveal the new
and great features of the offspring of the sublime
genius of liberty. La Fayette seems to me to be a

dwarf who can only, like the ants, plant a sting in the heel. His most faithful friends are giving him up. Perlet says of him all that is needed to open the eyes of the blind. He has always been his friend, but at last he sees clearly. All this is leading to great events; but all is foreseen and duly weighed; Heaven is for us.

I send my son a kiss; I love my son, and every day I earnestly pray the Supreme Being to keep him happy and virtuous, two things that are inseparable.

Pétion is adored by the people, and all good men. The good party is strong enough to conquer the universe.

XXXIX.

To her Husband.

Paris, *July* 5, 1792.

Do you think we are frightened, feeble, bewildered? Renounce your error. We are as firm as the Alps, as lofty as the cedars of Lebanon, and as calm as the still waters of a lake. Nothing can be more imposing than the union of the societies, and nothing more striking than the majesty of the mother society. Its beneficent ramifications carry strength and vigour with them everywhere. The National Assembly, roused with difficulty by the pressure of opinion, has just broken up the staff, and incorporated the French Guards in the National Gendarmerie; which, however, I should have liked better with their first name. A decree, of eighteen excellent articles, proposed by Jean de Brie, was passed yesterday. Vergniaud's speech, which I advise you to read, enlightens the blindest. A decree for the reception of the federals, sanctioned on the spot; corrupt ministers, a perverse court exposed to the light of day; an alert watchfulness in the expectation of a great event; such is our situation, and we are calmly looking on. Luckner has evacuated Tournay, and set fire to the suburbs of a city in which the French had received generous hospitality. This new atrocity will not impose on the brave people of Brabant, or the bold soldiers of liberty; they all recognize the barbarous game of the courts in the unrighteous deed. Luckner is a passive instrument; another is the soul of this base intrigue, all the facts of which are now laid bare. This is the second scene of bloodshed enacted by barbarous puppets, to stifle liberty. The defeat of Mons and the evacuation of Tournay have been contrived to favour the infamous policy of the cabinets; indignation has risen high, and perfidy is stripped of its garments. If the National Assembly does not strike down the unconstitutional general, he will have the effrontery to push this policy to the end. It is plain that his design is to place the court in the heart of his forces, to draw the corrupt part of the National Assembly to the same point, and from thence to impose fetters upon the whole realm in the name of the law. La Fayette drove about the capital with six or eight hundred officers of the Parisian force surrounding his carriage. It was Scylla in Rome. His last letter to the Assembly had all the modest arrogance of a despot. He regretted, it said, that the Assembly had not yet done anything in the spirit of his petition, and Ramond has surnamed him the eldest son of liberty. Collot d'Herbois said—as I have written to Jules,—" It is an eldest son who assassinates his mother; if he be our eldest brother, it is Cain ! "

The sections of Paris, the departments, the private petitions, all have uttered a cry of indignation against La Fayette at the Assembly. The journals carry the sound of that cry all over the world; lastly, the village newspaper, and Perlet, his two faithful flatterers, have broken their idol, and see the ape-Cromwell, or the dwarf-Monk, in the hero of the two worlds.

If to-day it be declared, as it ought to be, that " the country is in danger," I have an idea that you will hasten your return. I know that a citizen can render services to the country everywhere; but, nevertheless, I think your place is here, for the double reason that you are a supplementary deputy and a soldier-citizen. Uniform was put down by a decree yesterday. The present soldiers are not obliged to wear it, except at their own pleasure. Yours has been destroyed; you have not an idea of the imperious majority of public opinion. The demonstration of the people, their peccadillo towards

the king has been, as in the fable, judged a case for
hanging; and it is La Fayette who has come royally
to cry "*haro*" over the ass. "We are lost!" cried
the fools: "We are saved!" replied the clear-sighted,
because here is this man unmasked before he has
won the laurels of victory, which would have hidden
all the deformity of his open perjury. Although he
says "my king," as a pretty woman says "my
parrot," we have already seen letters from soldiers
who tell how copies of the king's proclamation to
the people were rammed down into the muskets,
so fallacious and destructive to liberty did it
appear.

Do you know, that all those great public interests
overpower the human "ego" in me to such an
extent that though I have a two-edged dagger in
my heart, your absence and your silence, I am hardly
able, nor do I wish, to speak to you of that. Nevertheless, I implore you, write to me! And come
back, *mon ami.* What a space, what days, what
moments have been subtracted from my life! Cruel
sister, how dear your interests cost me! Adieu!

XL.

Paris, *July* 7, 1792.

I would give anything in the world that you
were with me now, for my own sake, and because
of the interest I take in the commonwealth concerning which you would settle my opinions, with that

wisdom and penetration which have never deceived
you. Listen, and pay attention to this. The
directory of the department of Paris has this morning suspended the brave Pétion from his functions.
This news, as yet only whispered, is credited by
some, rejected by others, according to their desires
or apprehensions, and every one is floundering
about in an uncertainty which suspends all action.
I arrived at the National Assembly, with Auguste,
at noon. Brissot was to demonstrate in a speech
the necessity for prosecuting La Fayette, the court,
and the ministers, and bringing the perfidy of all
to the test of evidence. Vergniaud, Gensonné,
Jorné, and Condorcet had begun on Monday last
to prepare this last stroke; and all their speeches,
which no doubt you will read in the *Moniteur*, are
characterized by truth and vigour. A colonel in
La Fayette's force appeared at the bar and denounced him, with proofs. This colonel had been
obliged to resign because, having refused to affix
his signature to the famous petition, he was exposed to gross insults on parade. He added other
proofs, and an immediate cry was raised that La
Fayette should be accused, for within the last week
evidence against him and of general disapprobation
of his conduct had been gathered from all sides.
Colonel B—— was admitted to the honours of the
sitting; he is a fine-looking man, with a Roman
air. The Assembly and the tribune applauded him
loudly. Suddenly there sprung up at the tribune

other speakers. A man in a black coat spoke with
the unction of a missionary; this was M. Lamourette, of Lyons. He said that every passion ought
to be subdued, that the danger of the country
should impose silence on resentments of every kind,
that union originating in the bosom of the august
Senate would be imitated throughout the entire
realm, and cemented by virtue; that the astonished universe would contemplate it, and the
monster of civil war be stifled in the embrace of
brotherhood. He came down from the tribune,
and instantly reascended it, as though inspired. He
moved that they swear to execrate the two Chambers as well as the Republic, that they may kill
two factions at a blow.[4] President Girardin put
the motion to the vote, with the rapidity of light-
ning; then, by one of those incomprehensible
electrical miracles which make a vast crowd experience a strong commotion at the same instant,
the whole Assembly stood up with upraised arms,
and shouted, in wild enthusiasm, " Yes! a thousand times, yes !" Never was there a fiercer, more
exciting, majestic, and astonishing spectacle; I
was choked with rage, because I detected the snare,
nevertheless, my eyes were charmed, in spite of my
reason, by this sublime union unmistakably displayed. The deputies had their hats, and they
waved them in the air as a mark of approba-

---

[4] Lamourette's proposition ended in this manner. See *La
Révolution Française*, by Louis Blanc, vol. i., ch. xiii.

tion. The galleries applauded until the very roof
rang. The intoxication spread to all present. The
" blacks " came forward, a tumultuous movement
was made; the 700 representatives thronged together, changed places, and in a moment were
clasping and kissing one another. Lastly, Jaucourt,
Cheron, Dumolard, Dames, and others flew to the
Mountain. The waves of the tempest subsided;
all were changed, and sacred fraternity seemed to
unite and to transport them. The paleness of
Gensonné and Bazire, the noisy and malignant joy
of Gaillard, Fleury, &c., filled my soul with fear.
A motion was immediately made to support the
entire constitution. Lecomte moved that the word
entire be erased; then came another motion that
twenty-four members should be sent to carry the
good news to the king. They set off at once.
Brissot, speaking from the tribune, said gravely
that as he had to discourse of matters which
might revive angry passions, he thought it best,
considering the effervescent joy of the Assembly
at that moment, to postpone them until the morrow;
and the Assembly passed to the order of the day
upon marriages. The profound impression of terror
and distress made upon me increased so painfully
that I was obliged to go away. I was in M. Euvy's
box, with four or five other women. Several good
patriots were there, rejoicing; the surprise had
turned all heads. The succeeding events, which I
give from hearsay, are equally astonishing. The

municipality appeared and with generous disinterestedness demanded to share the fate of Pétion, and that all should be judged upon the *procès-verbaux* which they had brought with them, and which contained all the facts. They might have added that the crime of the virtuous Pétion was that of having saved 20,000 lives, on the 20th June, that day on which the directory of the department would have had them sacrificed for the good pleasure of a perverse court. Would you believe it ? By the terms of the constitution, this had to be referred to the executive power, which is called upon to make its report to-morrow ; on which the Corps Législatif will confirm or improve according to the forms of the constitution. The king is arriving at the Assembly : tremendous applause.

XLI.

PARIS, *July* 8, 1792.

Yesterday evening the square before the Maison Commune, the Tuileries, and the Palais Royal were filled with an immense crowd, demanding to have Pétion back again. At night bands of workmen, five or six in each group, went shouting through the streets that Pétion must be given back to them. To-day some of the sections went to the National Assembly to make the same demand. President Girardin succeeded in getting the petitions sent back to the committee, but he could not hinder

the roof of the Senate House from ringing with
that cherished name, and with this sentence : " Give
us back Pétion, and break up the department."
That is the general desire. To-day the king had the
Tuileries closed. He has written to the Assembly
that it was for them to have the dismissal of the
worthy magistrate of the people revoked.[5] The
Assembly has sent back to the king again, so that
the affair is prolonged. Pétion has had an address
printed—it is posted everywhere—in which he
enjoins order, and the quiet waiting for his re-
habilitation by the law : he has the wisdom of
Socrates or Aristides. To-morrow ought to witness
his triumph, and the overthrow of his enemy. This
is so firmly expected that it must be. Union produces a great effect by its hopefulness. The credulous vulgar admire, clever people fear, aristocrats
swear, all this makes a schism in their sect. If
you were here you would see farther than I do.
What I observe with satisfaction is that the court
walks, like crime, in trembling. They do not know
what they are doing. Yesterday the king ordered
his gardens to be opened, with all the cheerfulness
and loyalty of a constitutional monarch ; to-day he
has had them shut, with the caprice and ill-temper
of a despot. All this is not lost upon the observers,
and the public mind is not deceived, although
many cunning devices are resorted to. Paris was

---

[5] Pétion had been suspended from his functions as Mayor of
Paris by the directory of the department.

calm and bright to-day, as if nothing was the matter. Everywhere, however, groups were to be seen, quietly and firmly discussing the affair of Pétion, and loudly praising his humanity, his profound wisdom, and all his virtues. This true magistrate of the people has just published a pamphlet entitled, *"Règle générale de ma Conduite,"* it is virtue in doublet and hose, and truth with features which must strike the blindest. In short, yesterday, we were waiting for to-day, and to-day we are waiting for to-morrow. French impetuosity is becoming tempered by the Anglomania, and respect for the law is a powerful curb, whatever the calumniators of the people may say.

I have received letters from our Jules; he has written to you. Nothing new, but everything very interesting. He has seen Dr. Priestley, and is charmed with him. The doctor has the simplicity and the wisdom of Phocion.

The king's councillors made a fine speech to him in which they had the effrontery to say that this meeting was the dearest object of his wishes, and that they are all going to make the constitution, to which he has sworn, and which they desire to support, work smoothly. He left the Assembly; the Tuileries, which have been shut since the 20th June, were opened by his orders.[6] The people poured

---

[6] There is a discrepancy in the writer's statements on this subject, as the reader will perceive on comparing the reference made to it in the first paragraph of Letter XLI. with this

into the gardens in crowds; every one, they say, looks joyous. Shall I tell you? Three-fourths of Paris know nothing of the fate of Pétion, who is, however, suspended from his functions, and whose place is filled by another. The surprising events of the day bewilder the public mind. The street-criers deafen one. Great meeting of the National Assembly. The king came thither and embraced both parties. Pétion's warning to the people is on the walls of every street in Paris to-day. Let the people keep quiet; between this and the 10th, we shall see great events. The calmness of the people only can save the commonwealth, and respect and obedience to his advice will make them patiently wait for the *dénouement* of this great scene. If the executive power have the wit to repudiate the directory of the department what popularity he will acquire! and if he be audacious enough to confirm its crying injustice, what a touchstone for the meeting of the Senate! If this meeting be not an unrighteous work, the department will be broken up to-morrow and Pétion restored, or the day after, Paris will be in insurrection. The patriotic crowd believe in good faith because they are full of it themselves, and they flatter themselves, in con-

version. Besides, in previous letters, between the dates of the 20th June and the 8th July, she describes scenes that occurred in the Tuileries gardens, and herself as being present at them, and frequently alludes to the Tuileries as a place of public resort. These statements are inconsistent with the conflicting assertions in Letter XLI. (Translator's note.)

sequence, that the National Assembly is about to bring forth great measures, all favourable to patriotism, because of the imminent danger of the country. That may indeed be so, because the court and the bad deputies are afraid of the federals : all that is being done to-day is a mere comedy dictated by fear; the thread of the double intrigue escapes me. Do they think that they can sacrifice Pétion ? They deceive themselves ; we are on the brink of a terrible explosion. But, listen to this, and gather from it what it means. Yesterday, the Commune was convened extraordinarily for the purpose of reading a petition by an individual named Cahier, which is nothing else than the letter and the senti-ments of La Fayette against the patriotic societies, commented and expanded. This Cahier claims that the petition shall be presented in the name of the entire Commune, in order to make the National Assembly take the steps indicated by La Fayette for its dissolution. Pétion and Manuel as well as all the other patriots of the Commune, strongly opposed the said Cahier, who failed to carry his point by reason of the length of his petition and the strife to which it gave rise. The matter was adjourned until Monday. The department probably thinks that the effect of the suspension of Manuel and Pétion, will be to leave the victory to the bad side; but no! wait; I forgot to tell you that the Senate had decreed, upon the motion of Bazire, that all the administrative and judicial bodies of the

capital should appear to-morrow at the bar of the
Assembly, and all swear to act in the sense of
the constitution, and to maintain it with all their
strength.

It would take a great deal of penetration to see
through all that is taking place. I think that to-
morrow will be " the day of the dupes " for the
" blacks ;" for I cannot believe in the general corruption, and the lights have shone so brightly this
week that the darkness of crime cannot succeed to it.

XLII.

Paris, *July* 10, 1792.

Public events are so rapid and so interesting that
one's mind is always in a state of agitation that
interferes with liberty of spirit. I have been wishing to write to you for these three days, but I am
frightened at the abundance of my materials,
because I have not the skill of a good architect to
put them all in their proper place.

On Sunday I was present at the solemn farce of the
meeting of the Corps Législatif. I was in M. Euvy's
box. I felt the trap set for us at that moment with
all the strength of which I am capable ; and yet
I was enchanted with the beauty of the spectacle.
The unanimity of the movement to which the
motion of the priest Lamourette gave rise was quite
magical. Never, my son, have human eyes beheld
a finer sight than that was. How sadly did I say

to myself, why is it not the work of virtue? If it were it would indeed be a grand triumph for humanity. A spontaneous impulse moved all the deputies; a sentiment of fraternity united them so irresistibly that I saw those most inimical to each other embrace. So genuine was the cordiality that might be read in the faces of all, that the credulous vulgar must be pardoned for the readiness with which they fell into the trap. I wept with anger, and I was filled with admiration, because I knew that the mass was pure, and that the only criminals there were the small number of schemers who set these great movements on foot, for the sole purpose of securing an interested aim which they fail to attain, because Heaven defeats the policy of the wicked. And that has happened. The fine speech and the presence of the king, the *coup de théâtre* contrived by the traitors—the whole thing in short, has so completely disorganized the Assembly, that a majority for the good cause is certain, through the displacement of individuals. This happy combination destroys the harmony and the activity of the bad. Everything will turn to their confusion; the father and magistrate of the people will triumph with us. Our calm, amid this tempest, proves that we are worthy of liberty.

I have just come in from the Assembly, and send you the newest news of the day. The five ministers who appeared there yesterday and this morning to give an account of the condition of the kingdom,

M

and of the strength of our enemies, equivocated in a manner which could not deceive even the most· foolish hearers. They concluded their fallacious report by a sentence which was received with loud applause : " We inform the Assembly that we have, all five, presented our resignation to the king this morning." They were honourably accompanied by " bravos " to the door. Chambouas, the Minister of Foreign Affairs, was not there, having written yesterday to the Assembly to inform them that he was spitting blood. After this the discussion upon declaring the country in danger was begun. The opposition has succeeded in weakening and prolonging it. The Jaucourts and Dumolards have resumed their former place with all their aristocratic passions. I am discontented with the Senate. To-day, the sole advantage of the meeting is that Lacroix has obtained the vice-presidency ; all the rest was feeble and puerile. To-morrow, they may do better, for their attitude is very changeable.

Our good Pétion is still suspended from his functions. In the slowness with which this affair moves I detect the villainous malice of the minions of the court. Nevertheless, as all the sections of the capital demand him by hue and cry, so does the whole people ; I expect that he will come out of this the glorious conqueror of his enemies. His crime is that he did not have twenty thousand persons legally killed on the 20th June, for the diversion of a bloodthirsty court. In the eyes of certain fools the crimes of kings are peccadilloes, and the peccadilloes of the people are crimes. How right is La Fontaine in his fable of the animals sick of the plague : "*On crie haro sur le baudet.*" Poor people, how great you are in my eyes in your rude uprightness, and how little are these great men in their perfidious urbanity ! The crowd entered the Louvre accidentally ; at any rate this fault, if fault it be, has enabled us to make more than one discovery, and it has revealed La Fayette. The mask falls, the man remains, and the hero vanishes. A week hence we shall know what will be decided about him. All the hundred mouths of rumour accuse him, as well as the executive power, whose powerful protector he is. I foresee great events, and that the Senate will lose much of its strength by its procrastination.

Brissot's speech yesterday raised my spirits ; it sparkles with truth. Pray read the whole of it in the *Moniteur.* M. Talleyrand is recalled. Great reliance is placed upon the neutrality of England, although the sincerity of the Government is much doubted. I am afraid that the advantageous peace which it has just concluded with Tippoo Sahib may induce it to wish to join with our enemies. Be very circumspect in conversing with people in London, for I observe that free speech—the idiom of free men—is proscribed even in the very places where the idol of liberty seemed to be worshipped most enthusiastically.

All the federals, who are coming in crowds from the eighty-three constitutional parts of France, assert that the wine, wheat, and other crops have never looked better than at present. Providence loads us with its gifts, and lavish Nature covers the surface of this vast realm with riches and abundance which guarantee its prosperity. There are three federals staying at Montaigne, and twelve at Navarre. These three men of liberty have an air as proud and austere as her own. Madame Crouset remarked to me this evening that they looked as if they lacked *savoir-vivre.* "What matter," I replied, "provided they know how to die."[7]

On going into St. Germain-l'Auxerrois (the king's parish church) the other day, I saw a superb marble tablet, on which was engraved the Rights of Man, placed in the nave. This redoubled my devotion, and I prayed most fervently in consequence. As I came out I observed in the open space in front of the church, two men standing on benches, and surrounded by perhaps a hundred persons. Each had a catechism, questions and answers, upon which they were commenting with genuine eloquence. One maintained the aristocracy and the other the constitution. The latter had all

---

[7] The point of this is injured by translation. The saying is as follows :—

"Madame Crouset me disait le soir, ' Ils ont l'air de ne pas savoir-vivre.' ' Qu'importe,' lui ai-je repliqué, ' pourvu qu'ils sachent mourir.' "

the laughter on his side. He said things so quaint and appropriate that they were worthy of Mirabeau. A man of the people pushed me by accident, and was so eager to excuse himself that he walked on with me, begging my pardon. When I had fully granted it, he assured me that so much do the porters and *commissionaires* of Paris love justice and well-doing, that five thousand of them had signed a petition for the immediate restoration of Pétion to his office.

This is the people's doing, my dear, and we may judge it by the proverb, "*The voice of the people is the voice of God.*" That saying, as old as the world, seems to me to contain so great a truth that I regard it as the fairest flower of rhetoric.

The National Assemby has bestirred itself to-day. It has decreed that the king shall be requested to "pronounce" in the matter of Manuel and Pétion, who are to be restored to us to-morrow. It has declared the country in danger—the only means of saving it. Hérault de Séchelles did some Mirabeauism ; and lastly, several fresh petitions from the federals were received. These petitions recall so vividly the eloquence of Athens and Rome, and promise the country such generous defenders, that it is not possible to despair of its salvation. To-morrow the report of all the general's imitations of Monk will be made. On Saturday, the Federation, which will be superb and tranquil. But, my dear boy, do not talk of our affairs without the greatest caution, for it is the fashion for the aristocrats to fly to London. Beware of these deserters from France, and do not compromise yourself with them.

The Poles are beating the Russians hollow. Catherine will end like Louis XIV. Does not the jade know that fortune is feminine!

If we are ever under the orders of a patriot general, I tell you that Prussians, Austrians, Wallachians, devils—all will be beaten and conquered by free men. I fear none but French traitors.

The Jacobins are as majestic and as calm as though the cannons had no mouths ; they mean to silence them by the thunderbolts of public opinion. Collot d'Herbois spoke like a Roman for Pétion at the bar of the National Assembly. All the sections, all the societies, all the people cried, and still cry, " Give us back Pétion ; he is a good man ; he is a virtuous man exposed to the malignant darts of our enemies." Ah, the stupid Feuillantins say that we are bribed to join this chorus. All the gold of Pactolus would not suffice for that. Fools, imbeciles, with their yellow filth ! They think that all men are to be moved by that vile means. I am paid—I—to cry "Long live Pétion ! " Money is nothing, the public interest is all, to the party of the right cause.

XLIII.

PARIS, *July* 18, 1792.

I have not said much to you about our Federation,

because, although it was a fine sight and everything
was quiet, it was insignificant. I was seated in a
balcony of the Rue St. Honoré, to see the procession
pass by. There were fully 100,000 persons present,
but no proper order was observed. What pleased
me most was to see " *Vive Pétion* " written in white
chalk on all the hats. This cry, and that of " *Vive la
nation,*" were frequently and loudly raised, but,
must I acknowledge it, the *bourgeois* aristocracy,
to which the handsome and well-dressed women
who crowded the windows belong, did not join the
chorus of the good people. I did not see that enthusiastic concord which brings about an unbroken
union. I am not satisfied with the aspect of affairs.
The pusillanimity of our Senate and the foolish
credulity of the silly Feuillantins are really placing
the country in danger. I am less afraid of the
Prussians and the Austrians than of the accursed
policy of the moderates who paralyze the energy of
patriotism, and I believe that unless a miracle be
worked in our favour we shall receive terrible checks
both from within and without, through the im-
becility of the Feuillantin crew, and the perfidy of
their chiefs. The court is clever enough no longer
to put forward La Fayette; it is Luckner now.
He is at Paris; he has arranged with the court; he
is named Generalissimo of the Forces. He has
written to the National Assembly, and I remarked
certain phrases in his letter which clearly revealed
the man to me. My mind is made up about him.

My heart, which is the guide of my judgment, exposes Luckner to me; he is in truth a friend of the despots, and a dangerous enemy of liberty. The nation will not find out this truth, which I readily detected, for some months, and which I am certain I shall see slowly confirmed by able logicians, who have the square and the compass always in their hands. What harm he will have done, before public opinion has attained the point which I have now reached! The chief cause of the sorrow that fills every heart is that our poor soldiers are left to the slaughter: the wolf is shepherd. When all the inimical forces shall be mustered, the kings will issue a fine manifesto, in which they will demand the destruction of the Jacobins, and they will affix this trifling condition to peace. Judge of the clamour which the fools will raise! I tremble, in truth, while expecting this event; and if I did not firmly believe in the wonders of Providence I should be afraid, for the only secure rampart of our constitution is formed by the Jacobins and the people. Now the people are as unstable as the waves; they are as easily seduced by appearances as by realities. We incur, therefore, a terrible risk. The truth is that we are suspended over an abyss.

Reason, which Jean Jacques Rousseau calls that great vehicle of all our follies, operates very differently in each individual; for mine makes me see black that which my brother sees white, and his makes him see white that which I see black, while each protests his entire good faith. My dear son, in what a stormy time has Heaven allotted to us the few short moments we have to live! May it please Heaven to preserve us from witnessing the destruction of our dearest hopes. But, in truth, the irrational diversity of opinions drives the firmest believers to despair. Did not Cato the Censor add that one desire of his soul, "Let Carthage be destroyed," to every other utterance? So do I say about the great general. I reply to all arguments about the saving of the country by these words, "Let La Fayette be destroyed." It seems to me that all our ills are due to the magic influence of that name, and that his hypocritical love for the constitution makes so many dupes that he will have chained liberty, hand and foot, and gagged all its friends, ere they perceive the snare in which he is taking them. Meanwhile they are crying "*Vive La Fayette!*" in the streets, and his friends would have the people constitutionally killed to punish their boldness in proclaiming the truth. So complicated are the intrigues, so inveterate is the corruption, and so weak is the Senate, that I know not from whence our salvation is to come.

La Morlière has written to the king in the name of his troops, just in the style of the other generals. Thus, all the officers speak the old language, and conduct themselves as they did under the old *régime*; what is to be done with them? Nothing good, I say, and I fall back on miracles.

There is a commune which has resolved that the land of all its inhabitants who go to the war shall be cultivated gratuitously, thus binding itself to work for the widows and orphans. My feminine hope derives from this incident a strong argument in honour of humanity. Virtue hides itself under the thatched roof, and vice often dwells in palaces. Now there are in the lower world a hundred thatched roofs for every palace, whence it results that virtue is a hundred to one as against vice. Make a geometrical calculation, and a philosophical *résumé* upon this, and you will see that we, who value each individual equally, and who estimate him by his intrinsic value, must conclude, as we cast our eyes over our vast plains, that there are more virtues than vices here below.

The report on the great general has been made. His friends and enemies fought a battle over him for two days. It is decided to-day that a sponge is to be drawn over the past, because there was not a law. What blindness, what perversity, and what weakness! All this is tending to our ruin.

XLIV.

Paris, *July* 21, 1792.

I acknowledge, my son, that I am always striving to gain the mastery over myself, and I maintain that there is no age at which one cannot attain to self-restraint; because in my rigid watchfulness for some time past I have gained much that is essential in my conduct towards your brother. Our nature is so wretched that we must always fight with it; but it has so many resources, and such true greatness with all its defects, that with good faith and principle one corrects one's self, and may each day make a step towards perfection.

That *amour-propre,* of which one hears so much, imposes only on fools, and makes no dupes except of those who choose to be duped. *We know very well what to think of ourselves, to ourselves, when we like to look closely at ourselves.* Adieu!

XLV.

To her Husband.

Paris, *July* 23, 1792.

You do not then wish me to write to you about politics. This is, in truth, a great hardship, because I do not occupy myself with anything else, and the public interest is becoming so personal that one cannot help laying it to heart, as that on which hang our fortune and our life.

I bless Providence that our dear son has gone away from us. To Providence we owe it that he left us just at a time when there was nothing to object to in his departure; at present, it would be impossible. All the young men are enrolling themselves; I saw over two hundred do so yesterday, after a proclamation made by one of the magistrates in the section of the Gobelins; and the next two days, which are devoted to enrolling the volunteers, will see all the youths of Paris under the standards of Mars.

Since you do not wish to hear anything except from the journals, I beat my retreat, and will try to talk to you of everyday matters.

XLVI.

Your papa seems to be inclined to come back, and I have never more ardently longed for his return. He loves you so dearly, and esteems you so highly, that no father and son could draw the bonds created by Nature more closely than you two. I recommend you to place the greatest confidence in him, and to display the most perfect freedom in your relations with him. Your father unites reason and philosophy to the deepest feeling. Forget the paternal majesty a little, and see in him the friend only. Act in the same way towards me. The barrier of cold respect that fathers and mothers place between themselves and their children, chills love by restraining it. My child, we are friends, with equal rights, duties, and feelings. I defy a father, though he display the utmost power, to go more directly to his aim, for the authority of friendship is a mild and sacred yoke, to which the proudest neck may bend with nobleness and generosity. And what has that friendship to ordain? The virtue and the happiness of the young friend whom Nature has given us, whom Heaven caused to spring from us both that he might strew flowers on our path in our latter days. Yes, my son, you will be the glory and the consolation of our old age : strive for that, and always remember the joy with which the recital of a good deed done by our dear child will fill our hearts.

I approach political matters with difficulty, so grand and imposing are they. The murderous treachery of the executive power is so fatal to the prosperity and the glory of the nation that we are reduced to the cruel necessity of destroying it, or of wearing the shameful fetters which it is "constitutionally" preparing for us.

The National Assembly has just . decreed the permanence of the sections. Petitions for deposition are coming from all quarters. Public opinion demands that measure, and we are expecting a great event. To-day, Guadet proposed that a message should be sent to the king, conveying the strongest and the last representations ; all this is useless and trivial. Kings know no other reasons than their own interest, and no other law than their own will. There is no compromise to be expected from them. They promise everything, and hold themselves pledged to nothing. However, three years of perjury have not yet sufficiently instructed the unfortunate. French; the disgraceful evacuation of Courtray, and the atrocious firing of the place, which must render our name hateful among the peoples, those royal bounties which would be repeated at each epoch of this war, according to the infamous caprices of the court, have not yet caused all the scales to fall from the eyes of the nation. We are in the most terrible moment of our perplexity, and with a war on our hands which excites much alarm. Our levies of men have been so considerable since the proclamation of the danger of the country, that if all were under the direction of good sense, and the leaders were patriot officers only, I would defy all Europe to conquer us.

Robespierre's credit is declining; I always read his journal, but he is slow and incorrect. The incorruptible Pétion has privately written, " *Les Règles de Ma Conduite.*" I have read and re-read it. It might be the production of Socrates or Plato for that antique simplicity which is so much admired and so admirable. I must tell you, by-the-bye, that we have been so severely punished for our idolatries, that we keep ourselves within the bounds of simple esteem for the Mayor of Paris. Only the people who cannot manifest their love otherwise than enthusiastically shout vociferously, " *Vive Pétion !* "

A petition presented by Pétion in the name of the commune, that no further passports should be granted, was changed into a motion, and together with the sale of the property of the *émigrés*, voted unanimously. D'Averond has resigned; in short, the Senate is weak, and treads the path of our salvation only at tortoise pace. Public opinion is forced to assume a voice of thunder to obtain a wise measure.

Vergniaud is nicknamed "Barnave the Second." We do not know whom to trust, and we are indeed in great danger. I bless Providence for your absence. I would I were with you. Let us reserve our means and our energies for a more propitious time. At the present, the malignant spirit of the court has introduced the various dangers of the Tower of Babel, but of the excess of evil good will come. Patience and courage; we shall not be betrayed and tricked with impunity.

Deprémesnils, wearing a white cockade, has had the audacity to preach the counter-revolution in Paris. Yesterday, some of the federals and some men of the people attacked him. He is at the Abbaye, half-dead, if not quite dead. I have heard this news only confusedly, but it seems quite true. La Rochefoucauld, who has also resigned, has, it is said, taken out his passport to travel. The department is not filled up. If you read the *Moniteur* daily, you know as much as we do. It is rather amusing that there are editors of all parties for the *Moniteur*, and that it is good or bad according to the individual who has it in hand.

XLVII.

To her Husband.

My imagination plays me most trying tricks; sometimes your absence is an intolerable burden, and sometimes the troubles of our capital force me to regard it as a blessing from heaven. Yesterday the arrival of the Marseillais gave rise to an event, which it was feared would open the sanguinary door of civil war. Indeed there were a few people killed. The drums beat, trumpet-calls were heard, every means was employed till nine o'clock at night, and yet, in spite of all this, we went to the Palais-Royal and nearly to the Tuileries. M. Julliot, commanding a battalion of the Parisian National Guard, stopped us by telling us a combat was begun. We returned to the Palais-Royal, where everything was in the greatest agitation, and I came home again as quietly—except for the grief I felt—as you walk about your fields. I thought a great deal about it, and seeing perfectly well that it was a got-up thing, came to the conclusion that our side would soon get the better of it, which they did, and all our silly, noisy *épauletiers* have come back as they went. On the arrival of the brave Marseillais the National Guard of the Filles Saint-Thomas, headed by their commandant, provoked the new arrivals by wanting to make them shout, " Long live the king," and at the same time refusing to cry " Long live the nation." That was the cause of the quarrel, and the commandant was killed in the struggle by the Marseillais. He was an aristocrat. The consequences of all this might have been much more serious.

I am becoming so wilful and so independent that I own no master but martial law. Pétion is an excellent man. Last night I said to our good Marion, "Mark my words, nothing will happen to-night, in spite of the drums, for Pétion is there;" and the reason why I jest about that hateful law is because it will never do any harm in such good hands. Robespierre is losing all credit.

XLVIII.

PARIS, *August* 4, 1792.

We are in great political difficulties, my dear husband. The conflict between the Marseillais and a small number of the aristocratic National Guard, has been followed by no other consequences than the exposure of the perfidious schemes of those who wish for civil war; but I think the broad daylight of truth which illuminates this murderous project will confound it, or at least check it for some time. A frightful event has again excited our indignation. Our volunteers at the camp at Soissons have been poisoned by powdered glass being put into their bread. The report of the commissioners sent by the Assembly seems to indicate that it was carelessness, rather than premeditation, but that deceives no one. This crime makes one shudder with horror, and it is proved by the sufferings of about one hundred victims, who must perish in frightful agonies. The cruelties of the aristocrats light the torches of vengeance, and these barbarities in the eighteenth century afflict the humane, the philosophical. How glad I am, my poor child, that you are in a strange land. Be circumspect and philanthropic there; preserve your life, that you may one day sacrifice it to the sublime love of country. At this time of confusion it seems to me that self-devotion is perilous, without being glorious. Yesterday, Pétion, in the name of the commune of which he is only the mouthpiece, demanded at the bar of the National Assembly the deposition of the executive power, for breach of faith. This is the wish of forty-two sections of the capital; and the departments consulted will accept or reject it, as they think fit. Some say that such a great preventive measure would avert the danger of civil war, others that it would only hasten its explosion.

Sunday Evening.

Thank Heaven, my son, the disasters of Soissons have nearly disappeared under the investigation of the commissaries, and it has been proved that negligence alone was the cause of them. You will have seen all the details in the papers. We are very quiet in the midst of our storms. Petitions and addresses in favour of the forfeiture of the throne pour in at the Assembly. This great question, and the affair of La Fayette, form the business of the House for this week. You can imagine the crowd of citizens at the Senate, and the agitation of the capital.

I saw an Englishman to-day who wants to be a captain in our troops.

I am sorry for the decree which uncloisters all the nuns, although the religious aristocracy has been the cause of it. The Superior of the Grey Sisters of Reuil lost her pocket-book, and it was carried to the municipality of the place and opened there. It was proved by it that they had sent 48,000 francs to the *émigrés* since the 1st of January.

If you have read the official report of what passed on the occasion of the enrolment, you must have noticed the prodigies of civic virtues that are fore-runners of the great destinies of a nation which with such defenders will be invincible. I was at the National Assembly when the *procès-verbal* was read. Every one wept, both aristocrats and patriots; the women sobbed aloud. I was transported with admiration, joy, and delight; and in such generous self-sacrifice I foresaw the saving of the realm. Yes, my son, the French rise far beyond other nations by the elevation of their sentiments. Unfortunately, what elevates some, lowers others. A time of revolution developes all the vices as well as all the virtues, because conflicting interests are brought into play.

The terrace of the Feuillants is a splendid place for observers of the people, and friends of law and liberty. A mere silken cord defends the entrance to the Tuileries, yet not one profane foot passes that frail barrier. The superb garden is absolutely deserted, and the terrace is crowded with people. This is a sharp contrast. French wit amuses itself by slight sarcasms. "That is Coblentz over there." I have been there twice since; there are fashionable people sitting about the *café*, and groups of people standing and walking about.

I am going to the Assembly to-morrow; some women are going to present a petition against the general.

XLIX.

To her Husband.

Paris, *August* 5, 1792.

I must acknowledge, dear husband, that I think all our ills proceed from the pusillanimity of the Senate, or rather from the corruption of certain members. Pétion, the organ and mouthpiece of the commune, demands the dethronement of Louis XVI. This demand is supported by addresses so noble and so indisputably justified by facts that the opinion seems to me general. All the royalists here are selfish beyond everything, and would not run the very smallest risk to save a thousand monarchs. If La Fayette were previously removed from the army, Louis XVI. could be deposed without its causing the slightest commotion in Paris. I absolutely believe what I state, and it. vexes me to think that the Senate will not give me the pleasure of seeing my prediction verified. A properly organized executive power, obeying the constitution, would make all the kings of the earth turn back quicker than they came. For if, in spite of the treason of their leaders, the people flock in crowds to the frontiers, what would it be if they had confidence in their leaders, and if the forethought of a patriotic minister provided them plentifully with bread and arms, which are the only things required by free Frenchmen? Read the official report of Nancy. After such generous devotion what think you of the destinies of the country? nothing is wanted to work prodigies, and master fortune, but the example of a great genius at the head of our Senate. Then we should be truly a great people; but narrow views, selfish interests, petty intrigues, keep everything within contemptible limits. Poor Louis XVI.; it is to ease his shoulders of a burden too heavy for him, that I wish for his fall. The unhappy king is pushed into the abyss by false friends. In short, only two bold moves are wanting to upset the aristocracy completely.

The House will be occupied about them this week; you may imagine the agitation of the capital. To-morrow La Fayette : Thursday, his *protégé.*

1 am going to the National Assembly to-morrow. I went to the Jacobins this week, and came out at half-past nine, so as to get home at a proper hour. There were two or three hundred ladies there, dressed as carefully as if they were going to a theatre. I had not been there for three months, and it seemed to me that it was a case of lion's skin and wolf's jaws; but I mean to tell your provincials that the Jacobins are men, good soldiers; not at all *sans-culottes,* but the flower of the Parisian Bourgeoisie. They made a great impression by their virile speeches and their lofty attitude. I fancied myself at the Roman Forum. I heard Antoine, a former deputy, speak, and also Robespierre. It grieved me to hear them denouncing Brissot and Vergniaud. I always regret to hear people judge from hearsay. The Jacobins are the strongest pillars of liberty, and the terror of tyrants. But for them, for their energy and active supervision, and their public discussions, which rouse the people and excite their patriotism, the counter-revolution would already have rejoiced the hearts of our enemies. If they succeed in paralyzing the Jacobins, adieu to the constitution.

As you prolong your absence for another month, I think I shall go and pass it in the country. The truth is that I should like to get away from all the public agitation. I might shut myself up between the walls of my apartment; but the proximity of the scene, the interest I take in all that passes, a certain power of observation that I fancy I possess, all combine to attract me towards the theatre of these events, and I invariably bring from it fresh convictions of safety and security which make me bold. I want to breathe the country air, my dear husband, and not to think, or hear, or talk of politics for a time. Of the fifteen or twenty thousand young men enrolled and about to leave Paris under the orders of a general, who will perhaps be discovered to be the man of the counter-revolution, very few, I fear, will return alive; and I thank Divine Providence, which has exiled my son from a country whose sovereign sacrifices the young men of it to his own interests, because they would be the warmest partisans of liberty. Heaven will not permit the perpetration of such a crime ; our safety is written in the book of fate, and there also two lines are inscribed, which form the closing words of a petition that you will be sure to remark in the newspapers.

L.

To her Husband.

Paris, *August* 7, 1792.

A terrible storm is gathering on the Parisian horizon. To-morrow La Fayette's affairs will be discussed.

I should be almost tempted to go to the Senate were it not for my little Auguste, whom I do not want to shut up there for five or six hours.

Would you like to know my opinion? I think
the Senate is too weak to dare anything, and that
its weakness will cause a terrible explosion. This
oracle speaks more plainly than that of Calchas. It
is not civil war, but a sudden action on either side,
which will stun the one that gets the worst of it;
but no one can foresee the issues of chance, or the
sum of the general evil that may arise. The duration
of the discussions, judging by their importance, will
give me, I hope, time to be under your protection
before the blow falls. I repeat that my great fear
is to be the too sensitive witness of an unfortunate
catastrophe. I am sure the popular party will
triumph, but the others are also brave men,. and I
have a horror of bloodshed.

Yesterday I heard the magnificent petition, signed
by so many citizens that there is a great book full
of signatures. The young orator who read it had a
delivery worthy of Cicero. It was listened to in
perfect silence, interrupted only from time to time
by applause that was as majestic as the subject. The
invocation to the Supreme Being appeared to me
pathetically grand, and the entire petition was read
with genuine warmth of sentiment. The attentive
attitude of the spectators was extremely striking,
and the aspect of the assembly at that moment
truly imposing. When the reading was over, the
" blacks " made a tremendous effort to prevent the
admission of the petitioners. The contrast of the
noise with the silence which had preceded it, was

like the difference between a calm sea and a stormy
ocean. At last our party got the advantage.
Calvet wanted to speak; he raised a perfect tumult,
and stood out against the majority with as much
impudence as Dumolard.

I shall tell you no more, for I remember that
you do not like me to dwell on details. The deputies are like Milton's demons.

Adieu! I am no more afraid of the Savoyards
than I am of the Prussians and Austrians. I am
afraid of nobody but traitors.

The terrace of the Feuillants is my favourite
promenade. Deserted Austria forms a striking contrast to it, and the silken cord continues to be an
insurmountable barrier. Lately a lady passed over
it not knowing. They made her shake off the dust
of her shoes, with a playful gaiety which exasperated me against the calumniators of a people who
are always good, except when they are forced into
wickedness. I was there. . . . .

LI.

PARIS, *August* 8, 1792.

The horizon is laden with vapours which must
produce a terrible explosion. The cloud contains
a thunderbolt. Where will it fall ?

The National Assembly seems to me too weak to
second the desires of the people, and the people
too strong to let themselves be controlled by the

Assembly. From this conflict, this struggle, an event must ensue : the liberty or slavery of twenty-five millions of men. My activity and my feelings combine to take me often to the National Assembly, to the Jacobins Club, and to the public promenades, where every one talks of the present state of things. I have made such just observations in these different places that I can now see or foresee the future with a prescience that I regard as prophetic. The patriotic party will prevail, but it is unfortunately impossible that its laurels should remain for long unstained by blood.

The dethronement of the king, required by the majority, and rejected by the minority which rules the Assembly, will be the cause of the severe strife which is imminent. The Senate will not have the audacity to pronounce the deposition, and the people will not be cowardly enough to support the contempt with which public opinion is treated. On the army, in the hands of traitors, our enemies found their pride and hope; it is the army that will save us, for the soldiers of liberty can no longer be the satellites of despots, and the agents of their vengeance. You may judge from this what kind of events will come out of this present chaos, and do you not think that a woman and child, who are intrepid in the good cause, and who go everywhere to get news, are gratuitously exposed to danger ? I might remain at home or go to the country. Very good ! but I have a certain curiosity whose

source is in my heart and which directs my steps
in the direction of danger. The secret of the wise
is to know themselves. I am wise. It is easier
for me to fly than to resist. I have said to myself
a thousand times, that the sight of these troubles
and the struggles of passion, so violent at the present moment, is not good for Auguste's young and
tender mind. Reason has said as much on that subject as Mentor could say, and yet I am always
caught in the same trap; the great interest of public
affairs leads me to the political centre where we
take up things so warmly that we come home with
our minds exhausted with fatigue, and our hearts
burning with passion, longing for the morrow that
is to bring the continuation of the debates.

I did not go to the National Assembly to-day,
but I heard that the disorder there was considerable. The committee made the report on La
Fayette, and ended by a decree of accusation. The
discussion was stormy, but the vote was favourable
to him. Conceive the disappointment of the friends
of liberty! This is preparing another defeat for
them : I am certain that shame will be inflicted on
them. But all this only brings us nearer to a
catastrophe that makes the friends of humanity
tremble; for *I do not exaggerate when I say there
will be a rain of blood,* and as the importance of
the deliberation necessitates its slowness, we shall
pass another fortnight before the terrible blow falls
which will decide the fate of the realm, at least for

some time. We are in a more terrible crisis than all those that have preceded it, but we must not ungratefully forget the miracles that Heaven has worked in our behalf during the last four years. Providence shelters us under its wings, and woe to those who doubt it !

Would you believe that the stupid royalists pretend that the Jacobins are paid by the English Government to work for the disorganization of society, so as to bring things to such a state that everything may be annihilated. Every kind of extravagance is brought to bear on the minds of the French against the English. *Reasoning banishes reason.* Prudent men do not believe these idle stories, and the civil list of George does not do as much harm as the civil list of Louis. The latter corrupts everything.

Let me talk of you; that will rest my mind. What are you doing ? I long to know what progress you make in English, and whether you are getting used to the manners and customs of the country. Observe well : learn to know your fellow-creatures so as to feel for them the indulgent love that is always the result of a study of the human heart. That strange compound has been filled from Nature with so many conflicting passions that one must be both wise and clever to understand it. It is certain that we are born with good feelings ; and what causes our kind to be so calumniated is that the vicious minority attracts more attention than the virtuous majority. The latter, finding peace in their conscience, do not require to disturb the world in their search for happiness. One bad man makes a hundred times more noise than a hundred good ones. This is a truth one should keep always before one's mind, and it does the heart good.

Learn to ride on horseback, and to swim, if you have the chance. I advise you to develope your strength carefully, and to acquire frugal habits which will preserve it. Excesses of every kind weaken body and mind; for the sake of your mother and for your own happiness, which is what I have most at heart, keep yourself always under Minerva's shield. I do not wish to be a tiresome mother, always moralizing. I have to do with a friend whom Nature has formed of the most precious elements of my being, sensitiveness and love of virtue. With that I have nothing to recommend and everything to hope.

There is great excitement amongst the people; yesterday some "black" deputies were maltreated. We are waiting for a miracle from heaven to save us. Do not be anxious on my account, but think of the real grief we feel, and which is caused by the evils with which the country is threatened.

LII.

To her Husband.

Paris, *August* 9, 1792.

The tocsin sounds, the drums are beating, all

Paris is in alarm. The streets are full of people,
and the women, trembling at the windows, question
the passers-by in terror. What is going to happen ?
The dense population of the capital represents, to
my imagination, eight hundred thousand souls a prey
to all the agony of terror, rendered twofold by the
darkness of the night, and increased by every
external sign of alarm. Death can have nothing
more poignant than the anguish that fills my soul.

Friday, 7 o'clock.

Heaven be praised! the thunder rolled, but no
bolt fell, and the light of day has dissipated the
terrors of the night. I have been prowling about
my quarter ever since five o'clock; there was nothing
but noise last night, and nobody knows what cause
to assign to it. I am afraid that Pétion, who had a
narrow escape, will some day be the victim of our
ferocious enemies. The Marseillais, of whom people
are afraid, and whom they want to bring to blows
with the National Guard, the dethronement of the
king, that is demanded on every side, and the
acquittal of La Fayette, which has exasperated every
one, occasion an effervescence which will, without
doubt, lead to a catastrophe. I wish I was with
you. Not that I run any risks, but because the
apprehensions I feel for the people break my heart
and half kill me.

I have been up all night, and now I am sleepy. I
must tell you that we are greatly dissatisfied with

the National Assembly; they exhibit weakness
which will be our ruin, if the whole people, in-
cluding the departments, which must support the
capital, do not rise once more. A few courtier
deputies have been insulted and pursued by the
people—Dumolard amongst others. Although all
personal violence is very reprehensible, yet these
wretches, while demanding liberty, work so openly
to reduce the people to slavery, that if they are let
alone our government will be the most odious form
of despotism. They rivet our chains at their ease.
All those who have come to us from your province
are detestable, except, perhaps MM. de la Condamine and Archinard.

I hear the drums again : now I am truly pleased
with myself for having so generously consented to
put off your brother's return. Heaven never leaves
a good action unrewarded. In any case you cannot
have all my solicitude, and in every case you are
better off than we. State affairs are the affairs
nearest my heart, I think and dream of nothing
else. I see an abyss of evil in the weakening of our
party. Your private interest is bound up with the
general interest as well as that of others. Be
generous, and come to our help. The union of the
departments will be the salvation of France. The
court will play their game with us for the stakes
until they have ruined us. The court makes the
king preach the constitution, as the Abbé Maury
preached religion, laughing at it in his heart. I do

not pretend to be capable of resolving the great question, but here is an adage of the Abbé Maury's that I apply to it : "*He who wishes the end must wish the means.*" Adieu! I am going out a little, one must have quicksilver under one's feet now-adays, at such an interesting crisis; unless indeed one were cowardly and selfish, which I flatter myself I am not. I am prudent: I cannot be more.

I have not gone to the National Assembly since Monday, when I heard the superb petition of the Champ de Mars, and the orator might have been Demosthenes or Cicero, so perfectly was he equal to his subject. All Paris will be there to-day. Yesterday our stupid deputies made complaints. Messieurs the Inviolables wish to be respected, and we are quite willing to respect them on condition that they are respectable and not Coblentzists, for one must see and hear them to be able to judge them properly. I am dying to tell you—guess what! Quiet is maintained, but the *ides* of March are not yet past. Adieu!

LIII.

PARIS, *August* 10, 1792.

A day of blood and carnage, and yet a day of victory; a victory watered by our tears. Listen and tremble!

The night passed without disturbance. It was said that the discussion of the great question would draw crowds of people, even from as far as the faubourgs, for that reason the Tuileries were full of National Guards, and the Assembly had a triple guard. About six in the morning the king reviewed the Swiss Guards at the turning bridge. At eight o'clock he went to the National Assembly, the Marseillais came and united themselves fraternally to the Parisian Guards. Cries of " *Long live the king !* " were heard; the nation cried " *Long live the nation !* "

All of a sudden the windows of the palace were filled with Swiss Guards who, without warning, fired on the National Guard. The doors of the palace were opened, the hall was bristling with cannon that sent a volley amongst the people. The Swiss Guards were redoubled, the National Guards had hardly enough ammunition for two rounds, they were riddled with shot, and the people fled; but rage and despair rallied them. The Marseillais are so many heroes who accomplished prodigies of valour. They forced the château. The justice of Heaven smoothed all difficulties, and the Swiss Guards expiated, by every sort of death, the vile treason of which they were the instruments. All the royal family, playthings of a bloody faction, had taken refuge at the Assembly during a favourable moment. They were put in the shorthand writers' gallery, where they are still. Not a single newspaper has appeared. I have not heard a word about the Assembly, and, an unheard-of thing, they have perhaps been quieter to-day than at any other period of their existence. The counter-revolution was to have broken out to-day, 10th of August. Our adversaries, who are always fools, thought that by corrupting the chiefs of part of the National Guard, and by backing them up with the Swiss Guards and all the lackeys of the Tuileries, they could put a good face on matters, and bewilder the unarmed *sans-culottes*. Fortune declared herself in favour of the latter; the conspirators were confounded, and in less than two hours the Louvre was invested and the victory certain. The tocsin, the drum-call, a thousand sinister cries, "*To arms, to arms!*" re-echoed through all Paris. The shops were shut, the women and children hid themselves; no words can describe our consternation and despair.

The Commune has worked wonders, of which I cannot give all the details. Suddenly purged of its aristocratic poison, it organized itself independently of the directory of the department, gave arms and munitions, and seconded the action of the citizens, whom treason has so perfectly united, that cavalry, grenadiers, chasseurs, and *sans-culottes* are brothers, and all serve the public good in the same way. Pikes and bayonets have to-day effected a sincere and august alliance. All the officers will be degraded this evening, and since mid-day Santerre is the general in command of the National Guard. Manuel and Danton are charged with the Civil Guard.

Pétion is alive and well; but tremble! the king sent

for him yesterday, at midnight, to the palace; at five in the morning he had not returned. The anxious Commune flew to the Senate and obtained a decree to demand the people's magistrate. He came out escorted by some brave Bretons, and was taken to the Maison Communale, where Manuel reproached him severely for letting himself be kept from his post, and by the desire of the Commune consigned him to his own house under the guard of the courageous Bretons. (They say this was to make sure of his life and free him from responsibility.) Anyhow he passed the day locked up. It is thought that if he had remained at the palace, his head would have been thrown to the people at the first volley of the Swiss Guards. The people have broken everything in the château. They have trampled underfoot the pomp of our kings, flung the most valuable treasures out of the windows, set fire to the barracks of the Swiss Guards, and swear they will raze the palace level with the ground. Some heads were cut off, and there were a few popular barbarities, whose cruelty inspires more horror in the thoughtless than the refined and civilized crimes of the courtiers who sacrifice whole generations to the caprice of a mistress, or the pleasure of a rascal.

The French people have conquered Austria and Prussia in Paris. Two or three aristocrats that I saw hiding in their cellars told me that this was the day that would see them rally round the Tuileries;

it has turned out to be the one which has separated them from it by an insurmountable breach. They also added that civil war must now break out, but I fancy we have to-day extinguished the torch that would have fired it.

Louis XVI. is in reality deposed. He has suffered his satellites to arm against his people, nay, more, to fire on them! Consult the Constitution on that.

A courier has just arrived with some letters, of which the Commune has taken possession.

What struck me most was the rapidity with which all this took place. At mid-day the fatal fight was ended, and security, though not serenity, was restored. The women were all running about the streets crying and lamenting, because each was in the fearful expectation of some cruel loss. A good many troops came back about two o'clock with trophies of arms, rags on the ends of their bayonets, the spoil of the Swiss Guards, &c. Marion went as far as the Cour du Carrousel, where she saw them carrying away four dead, out of several thousands perhaps. They have not yet made out the list of the dead. She told me the streets were full of women; she had never seen so many people.

I have been out all the afternoon with Auguste, but we limited our walk to the Mairie and the palace; it was necessary to push through the crowd everywhere, and that prevented my going very far.

On my way I gathered details from a hundred witnesses of the firing on the people by the Swiss
Guards, which was so treacherous and unexpected
that it roused the rage of the lion, and united all
parties. It was not in any way provoked; all Paris
can witness the truth of that. I shall go to bed to-
night with my door open, whereas the householders
of the capital are double-locking their doors for fear
of robbers. That is their chief alarm, and there are
a great many persons who will be much surprised to
be alive to-morrow, because the *canaille,* who are not
arrested by the law are to come to-night and fall upon
them and their treasures.

Paris is illuminated, and the patrols are made as
in 1789. The profoundest quiet reigns here, and
the watch is so active that one can sleep in peace.
I heard them crying the evening paper at nine
o'clock, but I could not get it. I was up yesterday
till midnight, and I feel my mind worn out and
weary with all the emotions I have experienced in
the last twenty-four hours. It is midnight, and the
drum has roused me; they are proclaiming a decree
of the National Assembly in fifteen or twenty articles.
It was read in the Rue St. Jacques; I only heard a
word here and there, but from the loud applause with
which it was received I judge of its excellence.
Brave Marseillais, yours was the glory of liberating
France. Those valiant martyrs of liberty perished
the first, because they were in the foremost ranks.

The suspension of the king's power, the recall of

the former ministers, the punishment of the chiefs who yesterday betrayed their soldiers—treason that has caused the deaths of fifteen thousand men,—the primary assemblies convened, such has been the work of the National Assembly, according to the views of public opinion, and ratified by decrees. The king is at the Luxembourg, guarded by the people. Some admirable things have been done, and some frightful ones too. Some poor *sans-culottes* took back to the Commune all the spoil they had taken, and they have hanged one hundred and five robbers who had mixed with them. Several traitors, to the number of about one hundred have perished, victims of the popular fury. Well! that was a second revolution; the day should have been called the "Day of Dupes," because it was the one fixed for the counter-revolution, and because the following day was to have seen all the Jacobins of the kingdom drowned in their blood. I missed the National Assembly yesterday; I shall fly there to-day. It was from prudence and regard for Auguste that I made the sacrifice; I have thanked Heaven for it a thousand times, for I should have died at the sound of the cannon which roared all day, and the terrible political scenes which took place. I have a constant trembling, caused by the violent agitation that has shaken me in the last few hours. Adieu!

LIV.

PARIS, *August* 10, 1792.

Wonderful news, my dear Jules! We have a second revolution, as miraculous as the one in which the Bastille was taken, but which has cost us some lives, and kept us for the last twenty-four hours in a sort of frenzy, mingled with joy, despair, grief, and rage. Last night Paris re-echoed with the dreadful sound of the alarm-bell, the rolling of drums, and cries of "*To arms.*" The city presented all the horrors of a commencement of civil war. Daylight diminished our alarm, and calmed our apprehensions. Nothing had happened, except that the palace was surrounded, and the Senate protected. They were discussing the deposition, and the Assembly was inclined to treat the illustrious criminal as they had treated his protector, La Fayette. The deliberation was continued this morning, and the people, who had risen, were all anxiety to hear the sentence. The Henri Quatre battalion was to keep one faubourg in check, and at the château of the Louvre everything was prepared for the annihilation of liberty. At six in the morning, Louis XVI. had reviewed the Swiss Guards in his garden, after which they took their places in the palace, where cannon had been posted opposite the great doors. The National Guard occupied the garden; the Marseillais and some other federals, as well as part of the Parisian

army, occupied the Place du Carrousel, and the
Senate had a triple guard. The people were scattered
about as usual, here and there. About eight o'clock
the royal family slipped away secretly to the
Assembly. The king showed himself there. You
will learn all the details of this important scene from
the newspapers, and M. Euvy's letter. I know no
more except that they were put into the gallery of
the shorthand reporters. Let us go back to the
château, surrounded as I have already told you. All
of a sudden the windows were opened, they were
full of Swiss Guards, who, *without any provocation,*
fired both cannon and muskets at the people, killing
some and putting the rest to flight. The surprise
and terror lasted but a moment, the National Guard
fired on the Swiss Guard, but they had scarcely any
ammunition, and their enemies, who were well
provided, discharged several rounds from their post
of vantage. The tocsin and the drums called all the
brave men of the capital to the field of battle. The
Tuileries were forced, with the same promptitude as
the Bastille, and the unhappy Swiss Guards, guilty
instruments of the vengeance of the court, perished
by a hundred different deaths. The furniture in the
palace was broken, all the royal luxury trampled
underfoot, and immense riches thrown out of
window. The garrison of the Swiss Guards was set
on fire, and the flames devoured the dwelling of the
traitors. No words could describe the consternation
that prevailed while we awaited the result of this

great event, but we were not kept in suspense more than two hours.

Those heroes of liberty, the Marseillais, have become its martyrs.

This abominable act on the part of the Swiss Guard has turned the luck all on our side. The union between the citizens of every sort was so perfect, that the cavalry, all the other " blues," and the *sans-culottes*, formed a holy alliance of pikes and bayonets, which composed so compact and strong a mass that nothing could have resisted it. On this, as on every other occasion, some of the officers proved to be traitors ; they were broken this evening, and Mensard, their general, is in prison.

There were some popular executions which proved that the lion is roused. I cast a veil over those horrors, which my too sensitive heart cannot bear to dwell on. Yet reason makes me feel very strongly that humanity has lost fewer men by the gross barbarity of the people, than by the civilized rascality of kings and their ministers. In our imminent danger the Commune did wonders ; it is reorganized, the aristocrats have abandoned it, it provided arms for the friends of liberty, and watched over everything with perfect unity of purpose to assure their triumph.

This might be called the " Day of Dupes ;" for the counter-revolution was organized with the knowledge of part of the Senate, and now it is decidedly adjourned for a long time. We were so near being

put back into our fetters, that I look upon this unexpected event as a signal miracle, and sign of the
protection of the Supreme Being. He has helped
us to conquer Austria and Prussia in Paris; He has
strengthened the neutrality of England, and stirred
up the Belgians, the people of Liège, and our good
friends the patriotic Dutchmen.

All the letters received to-day were brought to
the Commune, and opened there. It is said that
among them are thirty-two letters from a general
devoted to the court and the king; these letters
will form thirty-two articles of accusation against
him, for they prove the design of the 10th of
August, a date that will henceforth be famous in
the history of our Revolution.

From mid-day until night the women filled the
streets, each in pursuit of the object dearest to her,
and when they met their husbands they would
throw themselves into their arms in the open street.
I saw many touching scenes, some grand, some
heroic. How many bitter tears I have shed, my
dear Jules, within the last twenty-four hours ! About
eleven o'clock to-night the drums made me tremble
again, but it was only a long decree from the
National Assembly, of which I heard nothing,
except that everybody at the windows was applaud-
ing and shouting *" Long live the nation ! "*

Saturday Morning.

My child, the Assembly has decreed everything

that public opinion demanded in that grand petition. The king is at the Luxembourg; all is quiet.
This bloody victory will cost us dear. I am off to
the National Assembly. There was a conspiracy
against the patriots, which would have insured the
death of the most active among them, and of a
number of Frenchmen besides.

LV.

PARIS, *August* 10. 1792.

The present state of things is not only the most
violent crisis of the Revolution, but also the most
astonishing and terrible blow that has fallen on
the monarchy during the fourteen centuries of its
existence. One fears to give advice, when one sees
that the most consummate experience, the most
perfect knowledge of history, the profoundest study
of the human heart barely suffice, even with the
help and support of genius and prudence, to trace
a safe path. My son, you who have received
from Nature a fresh and energetic mind; you who
come from the hands of the Supreme Being endowed with that fire of virtue, that ardent courage
which is, so to speak, the seal of real honours, but
which perishes in the germ if its development be
forced, remember that your age renders your advice
useless. However well inspired it may be, whatever wisdom it may contain, think how useless
it is for the public good, and, I might almost

add, how dangerous to yourself. But the strongest check for a son is the tender love of a father and mother who admire his budding virtues, and who hope to see them strengthened by his generous disposition, and developed by his talents. Hereafter, when you have acquired greater experience, I shall regard your devotedness to the country, as did that Spartan woman, whom you quote to me. Then, whether they bring you back dead from the battle-field, or whether you fall in the arena of eloquence, under the attacks of some powerful enemy, I shall say with that noble citizeness, *" I brought him into the world but for that."* But you are not yet fit to gather this palm of glory. You must work to win it, and not stretch out your hand to seize it, until by multiplied trials you have proved yourself strong enough to reach it.

The microscope of presumption deceives the keenest and surest eyes. It enlarges our perceptions so much that we think we have faculties and strength sufficient to undertake and do everything. The experience of others is of no use to us, and our own always teaches us too late.

At your age, a failure in a brilliant career often checks advancement, and unfavourably prepossesses against you those who pursue the same object. "He is a young fool ! " say those who are indifferent or easily prejudiced ; " he takes no trouble to get to the bottom of anything ;" and the faults of youth, or even those which are imputed to it, are

often and bitterly expiated in a man's whole after-
life.

LVI.

To her Husband.

When I consider seriously the evils we have
escaped by the triumph of last Friday, I feel so
terrified that I am ready to faint. Measures for a
St. Bartholomew were so thoroughly taken that the
miracle worked by the Supreme Being in favour of
the people becomes for me a sacred article of faith.
Tolle et lege. Such a mysterious conspiracy has
been exposed, that posterity will refuse to believe it.
If the tocsin and the drum had brought together
during the night the crowds one might naturally
have expected in such a state of popular ferment,
and in the midst of the darkness, there would have
been a hundred thousand people killed in Paris.
God did not permit the impetuous people to move
till sunrise ; the troops alone came and went without
any evident object, their leaders, who were in the
infernal secret, conducting them where they pleased.

Do not let any one persuade you that the reduction of Paris to submission by these means was a
wild project, because it appears impracticable to-
day. Circumstances are the masters of fools. The
failure of the court was attributable to the rallying
of the Marseillais and the Bretons, or rather to the

miraculous hand of Heaven, which changed the tide of fortune and forced the victory. The sustained firing kept up in the vast extent of the Tuileries and the Louvre, scattered death and terror. All fled. The National Assembly could not have held out a quarter of an hour. The monsters who had sought safety in its bosom would have pointed out their victims.

It is objected to this, that the provinces would have avenged Paris; and that the fear of the provinces entertained by the court, should prevent us from believing in the evil intentions of which it was suspected.

Poor people! how little do you know the human heart. Discouragement is a more infectious disease than the plague. There are plenty of cowardly royalists in the departments, who would have hoisted the *fleur-de-lys* all stained with the blood of the capital. The patriots would have fallen under the sword of the despots, and France would have been enslaved. Luckner and the other generals, with their forces, would have supported the triumphant party of the counter-revolution.

Fools regard this as the dream of a feverish imagination, but it only depended on a thread which was broken by a miracle of Heaven. I am like one of the National Guards of our quarter, who had a ball through his hat, and two of his friends killed beside him, yet who thought no more of it at the time than if nothing had happened. It was only

in the evening that he remembered these things,
and then it was such a shock to him that the bile
mixed with his blood, and he had such a violent
attack of jaundice, that he looks as if his face had
been painted yellow. That is what I feel, when I
think of all the dangers from which we have
escaped. The numbness of death seizes me from
head to foot, and I am obliged to rush out into the
street to escape the horrible remembrance.

There everything is so calm that I recover my
own tranquillity by degrees, but the imminent
danger which surrounded us, the abyss which
yawned to swallow us up, is ever before my eyes
when I am by myself. I really should have died,
if fortune had not declared in favour of the unhappy people. We are expecting news of the
troops. I am still afraid that some of the traitorous
generals may strike a desperate blow. I have gone
twice to the National Assembly since the memorable
Friday. They do what they can, but I do not consider them energetic enough, ... if . . . . but
. . . . I am dying to see you and hear what you say.

Wednesday Evening.

I have no news to tell you except that our army
commissioners—that is, the deputies that have been
sent to the army—receive a tribute of blessings and
encouragement on all sides. It is said that La Fayette, in a letter inserted in the evening papers,
has promised to use his influence with the soldiers

to induce them to receive the great news without disturbance; but I assure you that if my soul could have been in the body of one of the august envoys, I should have intrepidly seized the General-in-Chief by his collar, and have had him shut up. I tremble at all these precautions, and half-measures are as fatal to our enemies as to ourselves. To-day one should be humanely cruel, and cut off a limb to save the body. All this is alarming. They say Charles Lameth has been arrested by his own soldiers.

Paris is quiet. I have passed the afternoon in the king's garden. There was a crowd there going about in perfect tranquillity. They talk of a gathering in the neighbourhood of La Force, and of troubles at Rouen; they also say that a strong force has marched to Orleans. They are waiting for the court-martial, which ought not to act like the Châtelet. The Commune, composed of energetic patriots, is to provide for everything. The gaming-houses are closed; and since I know you see good newspapers every day, and that, thank Heaven! there are no more bad ones, I can tell you nothing that they will not tell you better than I.

So good-bye. I seem to have lived centuries in four days; and not having had a single line from either you or Jules I am very sad and anxious, though the evils that we have escaped console me for those we could not avoid. I have retained a profoundly painful impression; and feeling all the consequences of our situation, I am so afraid that the least advantages of it should be lost that I am only half alive.

I hope you will come back to me immediately. They say Chabrond is arrested. What surprising things revive our patriotism when needful. "*Liberty or death*" is our decree as well as our motto.

LVII.

Paris, *August* 18, 1792.

I have no personal anxiety; my mind seems to have a new being, and the great general interest absorbs all my emotions. There is something terrible even in our present tranquillity, for still watchfulness and fear keep us on the defensive, and prudence is ever on the look-out.

I went yesterday to the Assembly, which has certainly risen to the occasion. They are impatiently waiting for news of the army, and as the commissioners have been stopped at every step by the eager attentions of the people, they have not been able to send soon enough for our anxiety. It is even said that three of them have been arrested at Sedan. This last traitorous blow affects us without disconcerting us. We are waiting for more certain news to-morrow.

They say that La Fayette has gone to England, and they also say, what is far more probable, that he will be dismissed from his post by the Assembly

P

to-day. This ought to have been done on Saturday. However, patience and courage!

M. Servan arrives at his post to-day, and fills us with confidence by his active patriotism.

A hundred things come into my head; but as I do not want to write to you about the things you see in the newspapers, I try to inform you of those you do not see.

First of all, no persons of our acquaintance perished on the memorable 10th of August, and the number of those who met their death then is stated at three thousand; but if the party of the counter-revolution had got the upper hand, millions of patriots would have been immolated, together with liberty, throughout the kingdom. The king and his family are in the Temple. I have seen a commandant who was on guard there for forty-eight hours. These crowned heads have an entirely different nature from ours. They have no soul; they eat and sleep just as usual; they play backgammon, and do not even seem to think of a calamity which has filled us with horror. They are well guarded, but well served. Mdme. de Lamballe, Mdme. de Tourzel, Mdme. Babet, Mdme. Royale, the little prince, the waiting-woman, Madame Thilsot, and other domestics—the whole brood are there, and are always together. Two municipal officers sleep near the bed of the royal couple, who had thought to drown France in blood, and in whose eyes is yet to be seen the rage of hope.

As for me, my child, I have neither eaten nor drunk nor slept in the regular way since Friday. My soul is oppressed by a weight of grief. All this will be followed by important and terrible consequences, for which I tremble.

I forgot to tell you they are digging a wide ditch round the tower of the Temple, at which all the citizens work with the same ardour that animated them at the Champ de Mars. Those among the royalists whose minds are honest and humane, share our horror of that impious court. As for Madame Dejean, she feels just as I do about it; so you may judge by that of the feelings of a good many others.

Every day fresh proofs of the black conspiracy are brought to light, so clear and so convincing that they make humanity shudder. Be very circumspect, my child, where you are, for wherever the reign of the law is not well established, the free man must fear to fall under the stroke of agents of arbitrary power, who are all inhuman and treacherous. Preserve yourself for your country, which will more than ever want virtuous defenders.

The Jacobins, whom some fools magnified into extraordinary men, are no longer remarked in their club. They are scattered about in their sections, and I was told by a lady, who is one of the pillars of their society, that there has been hardly any one at their meetings since Friday.

The Rue de l' Observance is called and inscribed Rue

de Marseille. The section of the Théâtre-Français, takes the name of section de Marseille. I have heard, on good authority, that only thirty of those heroes, the Marseillais, were killed in the action, the rest are full of life and courage and are staying to form part of the camp of Paris.

The Rights of Man have replaced the royal bust in the Senate. I saw the statues that have been raised to glorify the pride of kings dashed down with all the coolness of reason. Even the statue of Henry IV. has disappeared from the Pont Neuf. The good often bear the consequences of the faults committed by the wicked and foolish.

I never walked so much in my life as I have done since Thursday. My observant eyes and ears are attentive to everything as I go quietly along with your little brother beside me. I notice everywhere, in the conversation of the people, a high and noble tone, which fills me with admiration for man in an almost natural state, and not yet corrupted by riches. The stupid bourgeoisie, of Feuillantin opinions, are surprised at not being pillaged and murdered, now that the people are the masters ; they have had, on the contrary, many lessons in generosity from them. My child, if there is virtue on earth, it is under the rags of those that have been branded with the name of *Sans-culottes* that you must look for it.

There was a little excitement yesterday, because the forms of justice are slow, and because the blood of our brethren still smokes and cries for vengeance. Our brave Pétion has made a wise proclamation, I went to hear it on the Pont-Marie with two hundred people. It had the effect of water on fire: he is right in saying we shall respectfully wait for the sentence of the law. The speech was received with tears of emotion, and bravoes a thousand times repeated, with cries of *"Long live the nation!"* filled the air.

And now, let them dare to calumniate the people! They will be great when those who conduct them have learnt how to teach them the dignity of man; a dignity that they defile when they are bowed down and degraded under the despot's rod. I hear them calling out in the street the sentence on five of the Swiss Guards, who are to be beheaded to-morrow on the Place de Grève. God grant it may not be soldiers who are to perish, for it is their chiefs alone who are guilty.

Charles Lameth has been at his country place near Pontoise for a fortnight. Clermont Tonnerre was sacrificed on Friday. I saw a grenadier, yesterday, who held him by the arm to protect him, and who witnessed his · unhappy end. They are arresting priests and relatives of the *émigrés*. The great desire is to break all the threads of the vast conspiracy, which, if it had succeeded, would have sacrificed a far greater number of victims than the Revolution demands.

LVIII.

PARIS, *August* 21, 1792.

My dear son, I am in a state of mortal anxiety about you. Where are you, and what are you doing? Why do you, who know so well your mother's tender solicitude and extreme sensitiveness, expose her to imagine all sorts of terrifying things about her beloved child. Your last letter, which is the ninth, is dated the 27th July. I know there have been disturbances in London, and I am afraid foreigners are not safe there. My heart conjures up monsters, and my reason contends against them in vain. I am greatly alarmed at your silence, my child, and the only thing that comforts me a little is the thought that, perhaps, at this critical time, letters do not arrive very punctually. I say that to myself twenty times a day.

It rains adhesions and approbations at the National Assembly. On every side, the great towns, the generals, the armies, utter the same cry, "Liberty! Equality!" These two foundations of our Constitution, which can never again be reversed, secure the eternal duration of the edifice. Some little changes may be made, the weather-cock might be done away with, and the building lose nothing of its majesty. What we wish for is the Constitution revised and corrected; the spirit and not the letter. The stupid Feuillantins, adorers of imitation, would have ended by sacrificing the substance for the shadow, and it is to save the country that we refuse to be the slaves of form. My son, we shall have another Constitution, and soon a new Senate, which will only have to lop off a branch of it here and there, without touching the trunk, to make it perfect.

We have been as quiet since the 10th, as if nothing had happened. Interregnums are moments of rest. Trade is flourishing here; there are numbers of foreigners in Paris and nobody goes away, so that the population is more numerous than ever. All are under arms. The Commune, the Senate, and the sections, maintain perfect harmony. The Jacobins are everywhere except at their club, because those true citizens have no further need of a centre, each having found his natural place. Their meetings are deserted, at present, as well as those of the other societies, which are in the same case. All the military officers are changed.

People are beginning to be anxious about the elections for the next session. We want just and courageous men, and as there is no longer any civil list to corrupt them, nor Swiss bayonets to kill such honest citizens as dare to proclaim terrible truths, the National Convention will have more than one Mirabeau. The choice will be made with more care, and less intrigue, than last year.

Madame de Lamballe, Madame de Tourzel, and Madame de Luynes were publicly interrogated at the Commune. The examination lasted two hours. They were considered so guilty that they were taken

to La Force. The *ci-devant* Prince de Poix was arrested at Passy. The number of criminals horrifies
me. The jury is organized, the new tribunal is
ready, and the people demand justice. They are
there, risen and standing in the calm and proud
attitude of strength. I was at the Mairie yesterday.
How gay and good-humoured the French are! They
scatter roses everywhere. At the Mairie there were
federals from the eighty-three departments. They
had tambourines, and danced *perigourdines, bourrées,*
and other strange dances with charming grace and
lightness; they were in the courtyard, and seemed
just arrived. It was their *débotté,*[8] and they were
all so strange-looking that they must have come
from the extreme corners of the kingdom.

If you could see Paris, my dear boy, and be told
of all that had happened on the 10th, you would
swear the thing was impossible; there is so much
apparent cordiality reigning everywhere, and such
an affluence of people who come and go and circu-
late with French activity and restlessness. Only
the men carry their heads higher, and look more
thoughtful—the men of the people especially. There
are no extra patrols, nothing to indicate any disturbance; there was never less assembling in groups;
in short, address your next letter to me in the
streets, for I so enjoy observing the public spirit that
I am running about all day. Tell Madame P——
that on Saturday I went to the Assembly and the

[8] Unbooting, or festival of arrival.

arsenal, walking slowly along the quays with your little brother, who is amused at everything and very useful to me. I look like a silly mother leading a spoiled child. I have wept and still weep for our martyrs to liberty, even the Swiss Guards who were gorged with money, meat, and wine, and made to believe a hundred thousand monstrosities. The really guilty ones are those who contrived and gave the order for these crimes.

LIX.

To her Husband.

Paris, *August* 22, 1792.

M. Julliot, senior, now member of the new department, told us all about his installation, which was very interesting. Patriotism is so warm and so pure that the four following things are to be sworn in the oath : namely, that the candidate has not been a member of a Feuillantin Club, nor a Monarchist Club, nor the Club of the Saint Chapelle, and that he has not signed the petitions against our worthy magistrate Pétion, and against the Camp of the Twenty Thousand. Two members were expelled for having committed this act of weakness, or rather of complicity with our enemies.

M. Julliot says that nothing can approach the intelligence and civic spirit of the composition of the department, which may compete with the Commune in patriotism. That Commune is majestically strong and imposing; it is provisionally composed of the best heads in Paris. The new organization of the officers of the National Guard is complete and perfect. The ministers who compose the executive power are filled with the true spirit of the Revolution; and the National Assembly, henceforth in union with all the constituted authorities, presents a most magnificent picture of concord.

The galleries are open to every one. No more tickets; no more abuses; no more favours. A brave citizen with a pike, or a brave National Guard with a bayonet says, " Pass, madame," to the rich and poor. A mind ever so little elevated feels how much this precious equality dignifies man. I spent the day at the Assembly yesterday, and shed tears of admiration and tenderness there. There had come from all points of France about three hundred addresses, thanksgivings, and adhesions. I looked for Romans in vain amongst them. There were so many, that they were obliged to limit the notice of them to the date and the place. The private petitions surpassed Athens and Rome by their warmth and eloquence. It rains money for those of whom the court made widows and orphans, on the bloody 10th of August.

I saw M. Servan present himself and receive the most enthusiastic applause with virtuous modesty. He said a few impressive words. We met on coming out, and I complimented him. He asked me with great interest where M. J—— was, and what he was doing. I told him, and added that Jules was in England, ready to do everything for the good cause that an intelligent and ardent young man could. He sent him a kind message, and added that his own son was coming to join him at Paris, and we parted. I cannot tell you how quiet and safe the capital is. It is not the degradation of servitude, like the morrow of the massacre of the Champs de Mars, the remembrance of which will never leave either my heart or my head; it is the quiet, wholesome movement of a free people, and the manly attitude of men who feel that they are men, and not slaves.

Vaublanc has not reappeared; Dumolard is in hiding. Public opinion has decided that the National Convention must be composed of chosen men. The cannon of the Tuileries will cause the Convention to be as good as the cannon of the Champ de Mars caused the Assembly to be bad. In short, we expect to have none but incorruptible men, and Mirabeaus. No more weak creatures; the hermaphrodites have been the cause of all our misfortunes.

Wednesday Afternoon.

Nunc dimittis servum tuum. My breast is no longer oppressed; my heart is relieved of a mountain weight. I have grown a foot. My dear husband, my prayers to God are all praises. I prostrate myself and cry with rapture, " Thou hast saved the people ! Thou hast saved the people ! " You and I, dear husband, whose souls are truly great and humane, we feel that it is sometimes necessary to be barbarous from virtuous motives. Those poor petty creatures who can only understand partial justice, are revolted at the horror of a head on a pike; the sight chills their hearts, and they cannot see that such a crime—perhaps a necessary one—spares the shedding of torrents of blood.

Yesterday, the perfidious D'Auglemont, the notorious suborner, took his head to the guillotine; to-day it is the turn of the Prince de Poix, and La Porte, the intendant of the civil list. E—— is gone to Normandy, as flat and as foolish as most of our aristocrats. He did not dare to speak up at our house; he thought himself as good as dead. It was in vain I tried to comfort him; the idiot was convinced that the people's victory would be followed by pillage. He will have been much surprised to find himself alive on the morrow, though I guaranteed that nothing would happen to his life or his property, and offered to be surety for them at any price he liked.

I went through the Tuileries yesterday, where they are preparing a funereal spectacle for Friday. At the foot of the great staircase there is a mere rail, and a written paper: "*People, respect the law, the seal is here.*" Several thousand individuals came to the place, and not one profane foot advanced beyond it. The public spirit is so firm and elevated, that in every street in Paris one might think one's self in the Roman Forum. The poor creatures who go about trembling for their precious lives, and whom the approach of a beggar soils or offends, will never know how to appreciate the people.

I went, dear husband, with Auguste and two thousand persons to the Pont-Marie to hear Pétion's proclamation; if you could have heard the jests, the remarks, the reflections, you would have been surprised and touched by the sensibility and justice of these good people who are calumniated so audaciously.

We have this moment heard that La Fayette has emigrated with his staff. He has gone to England, by way of Holland. The misguided soldiers, who, without knowing it, served him against their brethren, have at last had their eyes opened, and our commissioners are set at liberty. The National Assembly continues to save the country; they have to-day crushed the monster of stock-jobbing, by subjecting the public bonds payable to bearer to costly registration. Yesterday a certain D'Egremont, a suborner for the *émigrés*, was executed. The Prince de Poix, D'Affri, and La Porte are to be judged. The people are calm. Their victory has destroyed the civil war by crushing the venomous hydra of despotism. Thus, this degraded populace (according to the stupid bourgeois) have made us free and happy. Thus, the Marseillais, whom so many wilfully blind still qualify by the name of " brigands," have broken the sword of despotism that hung suspended over our heads.

LX.

M. Servan has recalled Luckner to-day, and put Kellerman in his place; Biron is named general, in the place of I do not know whom. Thus, my dear boy, I am easy as to the civic spirit of our armies, of whom the chiefs alone were to be feared. Everything goes on here with such sublime harmony that the most entire confidence and the profoundest tranquillity are the results of it.

M. Euvy sent me the letter you wrote him, this morning. If you really knew, dear Jules, what a father and mother Heaven has given you, you would not, for one moment, doubt their sanction to all the desires of your heart. Have I not read in it, dear child, the painful sacrifices you have made to my maternal love and its thousand tender anxieties! I am neither weak nor pusillanimous, and Heaven is my witness that if I had not feared the dastardly treason of those who were at the head of affairs, I should have reproached myself eternally for sending you away under the circumstances. But your youth and inexperience, the ardour of your soul, and the weakness of your body all combined to render it impossible for me to bear the idea of your taking military service, for I was sure that your chiefs, on discovering the ardour of your civic spirit, would have chosen the object of my tenderest affections as their victim. How many tears have I shed for the fate of those young and generous lovers of liberty, whom I saw enrolling themselves under the banners of generals that were traitors to their country. I said, those are martyrs going to seal the most noble of causes with their blood, but the cause will get no advantage from it because they are led by a traitor. Luckner is an old slave of the despots; he is weak and false, and unworthy to command free men. M. Servan has done well. He has struck a great blow without hesitation.

My child, my arms are held out to you. It was I who sent you into exile; it is I who summon you to return. I am doubly happy to recognize in my son the filial piety of Æneas, in spite of the impetuosity of Achilles. You may set out so soon as you receive my letter. I am so proud of the reasons that bring you back, that I shall not put any obstacles in your way, however ardent your civic spirit may be, for after having so many proofs of your prudence, I am sure it will never abandon you.

The people made straw figures of D——, R——, and Henry, and after carrying them through the streets of Romans, with insulting papers fastened on them, they burnt them at the toll-gate. Your father was at Voiron. This is a good lesson for traitors. It is said that Barnave is in prison at Grenoble. I imagine that the new *émigrés* will go to London, as the former ones went to Coblentz; that will render a sojourn in England both dangerous and disagreeable for true patriots.

I went to the Temple this evening, where the *ci-devant* king is shut up. The two towers are lofty, and present the appearance of a fortified castle; the one he occupies is on the side. The zeal and watchfulness with which the approaches are guarded are truly admirable. The horror inspired by the crimes of the court, has made every guard an Argus. Louis is indifferent to his disgrace, and she who has brought him to it is as haughty as Agrippina. Besides, they still hope to be delivered by foreign arms.

Friday Morning.

I must tell you that all our constituted authorities agree perfectly. The sittings of the Commune are of the greatest interest. The crowd of spectators is so great that it is impossible to find a place there. I went yesterday, but in vain. The department is public, so you may depend we shall have a National Convention composed of chosen men. Public opinion points to the purest and most ardent patriots. One thing alarms me; it is, that the forms of our new justice are so mild, that those who are morally guilty will not be considered materially so, and will escape the sword of the law. The irritated people will see their most just vengeance escape them, and that might produce a popular convulsion; but Heaven is there to protect us.

We watch closely. Every point of the capital offers innumerable proofs to observing eyes of the elevation to which this second revolution has raised the minds of the people. We cannot go any way but upward henceforth.

LXI.

To her Husband.

PARIS, *August* 25, 1792.

I know that Jules has written to Pétion, Condorcet, and Brissot. He has opinions and nerve. His letter to Brissot, which he submitted to M. Euvy's criticism, leaving him free to send it or keep it, appeared to the latter so excellent and wise, and expressed in such a singularly noble style that he thought it would enlighten Brissot's mind. He attacks and combats him with the modesty of a young man, and the firmness of a Cato, and with such delicate tact, that he proves his errors to him without offending him. At least that is the judgment of his friend, for I know nothing more.

M. Servan struck a great blow yesterday, by recalling Luckner and putting Kellermann in his place. All those who are wise cry, Bravo! and I am far from sharing the foolish alarms of those who fear the army will be dissatisfied. Luckner blew hot and cold; he is a base friend of the despots. He made two journeys to Paris, and paid his court assiduously at the palace of the Tuileries, but contented himself with sending his respects to the Corps Législatif. And then his indulgence for Jary, and his evacuation of Courtray, and in all his correspondence, his

Q

marked friendship for our enemies, his shameful disavowal of certain things which he has said! He is an old rogue that they have done well to expose. Biron is also a general-in-chief as well as Dumouriez, and they inspire confidence which is founded as much on their interest as on their patriotism. Montesquieu is on the same line. Our armies burn with civic spirit, and the accounts of the commissioners to which I refer you prove it. Longwy is attacked. News is impatiently expected. A little victory there would greatly add to our success, and such is the public spirit, that even a defeat would only redouble our courage and our hopes. Never, my dear husband, no, never have you seen a time of more strength and security. At every point Paris is a scene of calm and tranquillity. Little partial disturbances seem designed by Providence to consolidate and strengthen the good cause. The people are disturbed for a moment: a deputy appears in the midst of them, speaks the language of reason, invokes the Law, and everything becomes orderly again. The obstinacy of the priests and the nuns is the cause of these little troubles, which are dissipated by the breath of a legislator; in short, everything is going on well. The timid are still afraid of the struggle between the constituted powers, who, in the shock, strike against each other sometimes, but woe to those moles who see but one point. It is true that the Commune seems hard to manage, but there are conciliatory powers, and looking at things from above them, it is easy to see that they all follow the same direction.

The intendant of the civil list, La Porte, received the reward of his crimes yesterday. This is the second condemnation to death. D'Affry got out of it, by swearing that he had refused to give any orders on the 10th, although a very influential person of the court had begged him to do so. His defence was well received, and I did not hear any demur to his justification.

The National Convention is being prudently prepared. The walls are covered with notices and indications of the means of making good selections, for on that, they say, our safety depends. The noblest Republicans are already noted. We need Romans.

Cara is named guardian of the National Library, in conjunction with Champet. Public opinion is consulted and followed.

The six ministers work well and rapidly. Yesterday I heard six despatches of M. Servan's read. There is some confused talk about a bouquet presented to Louis XVI. by the Faubourg St. Antoine. There are none, now, but good newspapers and broadsheets.

LXII.

To her Husband.

Paris, *August* 26, 1792.

Little storms are blowing in the teeth of the vessel

of the state, and against the barques which provision
and protect it. The Commune of Paris, the Corps
Législatif, and the new department, are rivals for
precedence, and the enemies of the public good,
rejoice with the stupid Feuillantins, as if slight
discords between men, assembled together in a new
order of things, was not the most natural and the
inevitable effect of our miserable human nature.
Everything turned on the imperative demand
by the Commune that the department should take
the name of Administrative Assembly, and the
Senate does not wish that. Thereupon there is a
provisional state of things, and the matter is
referred to the National Convention, and all this
plants a little germ of discord, whereat the malignant
rejoice.

There is a great fuss made about the formula of
the oath, which excludes those who have signed
petitions, and frequented unpopular clubs. That
condition is looked upon as a refinement of Jacobin
vengeance, and the effect of hateful passions. I told
the Fessards, yesterday, that they deserved to be
flogged with all the whips of despotism for arguing
in that way, for if even such a measure were the
effect of the blindest passion, it is sanctioned by the
fact that it preserves us from those untrustworthy
men who had brought us within an ace of our ruin.
Is it not in this respect the result of the most
marvellous prudence, and can patriots permit themselves to assign any other cause to it ?

My dear husband, I should feel great pity for the species called man, if I were not your wife, and if you were not *my man* in the sublime and moral sense of the word. I saw La Condamine yesterday. He reprimanded the Commune as a schoolmaster might have scolded his pupils, and complained of the city of Paris, whose influence, he said, was tyrannical. Poor people ! I said to him distinctly, " The represented have saved the representatives, and this result might naturally give to the former a certain confidence in their views and actions. The Assembly should do them that justice, for it was they whose faults brought us to the brink of an abyss, into which we should inevitably have fallen, but for the strength of public opinion."

Sunday Evening.

All Paris is going to-day to the funeral ceremony at the Tuileries, which is beautiful and magnificent, but sad and mournful. I have already seen several persons who witnessed it, and at this moment—ten o'clock at night—it must be in all its pomp. There is an illumination and an excellent band. The unity and good-will of the people are manifested by their orderly conduct, and cries of " Long live the Nation ! " which rise to heaven. You will see in the Gorsas' paper a description of the order of the pro- cession, which took two hours to pass.

Longwy is taken. The garrison came out with the honours of war, but where was our army ? This looks like treason, and savours strongly of the Austrian Committee, which, although shut up in the towers of the Temple, may have influenced the event, for they had taken their measures previous to the imprisonment, and it is not always possible, at the last moment, to obviate the consequences of treachery. The defeat has roused rather than discouraged us, and the results may prove that I am right.

I always try to tell you such things as you are not likely to see in the papers, and what you certainly will not see in them is the alternate calm and agitation of the capital, which is one of its distinctive features. There is no uproar, but an extreme activity, and all the streets, the squares, and public places are filled with soldiers. The aristocrats go to the sections in the disguise of patriots, and but for the lucky oath that public servants are obliged to take, another insurrection would become necessary to tear them from the places they would get possession of by perjury. This is what the idiotic toleration of superficial minds would bring us to. May God preserve us from these things and their consequences !

The court party is in great alarm, for the crime of the conspiracy is so extended, so clearly proved, and so frightful, that one half of it is hidden from us, that the fury of our just vengeance may be kept within bounds. On every side the recall of that old humbug Luckner is approved, and it makes no sensation either here or in the army.

We hear very little now of Pétion, which is very strange; the Commune thinks him too easy, and he seems to live in a state of glorious inaction. The people at the Temple, and their guilty friends, are expecting the Russians at Paris in less than a fortnight, and we are laughing at them. I expect there will be some valiant deeds done on the frontiers, which will make them turn tail and go home again. Paris is becoming a second Rome; everybody is armed to the teeth; the camp is being rapidly got ready, and the town looks like a fortified place. More than ten thousand federals are reported to be assembled here, but in our peaceful faubourg we know nothing, and passing the day at the Luxembourg is like having one's head in a bag.

Our primary assemblies will give us good electors, and our electors good deputies. Andouin will be one of them. They say that walls have ears, one might add that they have tongues too, for all our walls proclaim the best means of composing a good National Convention, on which will depend the safety of the country. If our present legislature had a second edition as weak as itself, what would become of us? for in these last few days they have done and undone so many things that a child in politics might have acted as well. Nevertheless there is plenty of brains, and plenty of patriotism, but very little harmony in action.

LXIII.

PARIS, *August* 27, 1792.

I am well aware that all danger is not past, but there is only one that the brave can fly from without shame, and that is treason. There are, however, no traitors left, and now I can breathe freely, for hitherto I was always picturing them with their knives at the throats of the patriots.

There are still a few clouds on our horizon, little discussions between the Senate, the Commune and the new department, resulting from the bringing together of a multitude of men ; but as they are all following the same direction, a little jostling of each other on the revolutionary road can do no harm. The superb funereal fête at the Tuileries took place to-day, magnificent processions and decorations, illuminations, music, everything perfect. What touched me beyond everything was the kindly spirit of the people. They are their own police, and the perfect order and quietness they maintain render these meetings harmless. By an accident which greatly vexed me, I did not go, and but for that I should have sent you an account of the scene, on which I should have liked to have seen your tears falling. An amusing circumstance is that Jeannette, the Abbé's housekeeper, and an aristocrat by the grace of her confessor, came back from the fête converted. The harmony and concord of the meeting, the unanimous cries of " *Long live the Nation,"* the touching beauty of the ceremony, all combined to " disaristocratize " her. Amen.

The taking of Longwy is the corrective element in our prosperity. I have a notion in my head that the Prussians were drawn to the place by a thread of the broken web of conspiracy. We are distressed by it, but not discouraged, for we shall soon make them turn back, and the Poles are so exasperated with the King of Prussia, who has worked their ruin with that malevolent old witch Catherine, that I am in great hopes they will come and help us to beat him. A long time ago Mirabeau told us that the king was a fool, but for my part I rather think he is, like many others, a wicked, malicious monster, who devours men as greedily as did Homer's Cyclops.

I am anxiously waiting for the result of the elections. The frightful difficulty of our situation, if we do not fall into capable hands, fills me with alarm, but hundred-mouthed rumour indicates the line of conduct we should follow. All the vast extent of the walls of the capital is covered with precepts, the means to be employed, the measures to be taken, and reflections on the importance of a wise selection. Aristocrats and patriots go to the elections together, everybody is afoot, but the tares will be separated from the wheat, as the New Testament says. We run great risks, however; the cannon of the Tuileries has had an effect contrary to that of the cannon of the Champ de Mars, for whereas the latter killed honest legislators, the former resuscitated them, and, like the phœnix, Mirabeau will spring up afresh from his ashes. The calm that reigns in the capital is only equalled by its agitation. The problem resolves itself; for these two opposites proceeding from one and the same cause, exist together without offering anything to the mind except an admirable contrast, or to the heart, except pleasant harmony. If you are an observer of men, you will have noticed that fortune always attaches them to the victor's car, and that one brilliant example suffices to attract thousands. That is what has happened to us. The number of patriots is quadrupled, and because one deputy gave his cross of St. Louis for the widows and orphans of the 10th, they now fall on the bureau from men's button-holes by dozens. Men, being naturally imitators, should always look for good examples.

I think the Senate should be left in Paris, for this reason; Paris is the centre of intelligence, and gives the impulse to all the rest of the country; yet a set of fools are clamouring to have it removed elsewhere; in order to secure, they say, more calm and tranquillity for it. I am telling you things, my son, that you must have read in all the papers, but it may be news to you that Dumas himself acted the patriot, and unhooked his little saint to make an offering of it on the altar of the country. D'Averons has shot himself; Jaucourt is arrested. Vaublanc has not reappeared; Dumolard is silent; Chéron no longer thinks himself indispensable; and finally, to end their doleful story, the people at Romans made three straw figures of three of the colleagues of these cringing gentlemen, with "*traitors to the country*" pinned on their backs, and after carrying them through the streets, they burned them in front of the church of the Minimes. That does no harm to the body, but plenty of good to the heart, when one has any. It is a pity for them and for us, that they should have conceived the notion of becoming legislators.

Adieu, my son. If you wish to be good and happy, control your passions, and keep down your self-love, for these are the Scylla and Charybdis of most men.

Pons of Verdun is public prosecutor. Cara is at the Library.

Louis sleeps and meditates like Vitellius; Médicis is as haughty as Agrippina; they are waiting for the Prussians and Austrians to come and bring this *canaille*, wrongly called *men*, to their senses. D'Aigremont, the suborner; La Porte, intendant of the civil list; and Durosoir, the journalist, have left their heads on the scaffold. D'Affry (the father) was acquitted, he is eighty years old. Six hundred Federals have started for Orleans to-day to make sure of the Orleans criminals, and a new tribunal is organized.

The English ambassador is gone. What is M. Chauvelin doing?

LXIV.

In the event of my letter reaching you, you will learn from it all about our situation. The taking of Longwy has so roused the courage of our enemies that their insolence is extreme. The invading army is expected at the gates of Paris in a week. All the frontier towns are to behave like Longwy, and many other foolish things are to happen into the bargain. I felt, with all the patriots, genuine consternation and indignation on hearing Frenchmen express impious wishes against their own nation.

Danton, Minister of Justice, represented to the Senate the danger the country is in, and the necessity for the people to be always ready; also that prompt measures should be taken. He said that while honourable persons had vainly solicited passports, criminals had obtained them by bribery. Finally it was decreed that all houses should be searched in the name of the law; such arms as were not in use seized, and the names of those who had emigrated ascertained. The decree was made at three o'clock, at six or seven the drums beat the assembly. All Paris was roused, the streets were illuminated, the patrols were making their rounds, the women were at the doors, and at midnight more noise was to be heard in the streets than at noon on a *fête* day. Sixty thousand Prussians are devastating our frontiers; there are more traitors and more treasons, so we must remain on guard until they are vanquished and driven out.

Nothing could be more favourable to the popular cause than the mad presumption of our aristocrats. The most profound calm has reigned, and trade continued as brisk as usual, except in passports. The day was tranquil, but two hours sufficed to put everything in motion. To see the drums and the arms in the streets, and the vast population of the capital so serenely gay, one would think it was a public *fête* they were preparing for, and not a war.

I can hear them chatting and laughing on every side, and I am waiting in peaceful security for the visit of those brave patriots who are coming to disarm me. I shall give them your papa's gun with all the better grace that for the last fortnight I have been contemplating sending it to headquarters. Our aristocrats, who are brave in words only, and who, when the searchers arrive, will all be hiding in their cellars, will be modest and mum enough tomorrow, but if their dear Prussians gain another victory, they will recommence their bragging, and I do not know what will be the end of it, for the most forbearing patience wearies of their bluster.

La Fayette's three months of inaction on our frontiers has been the cause of all our calamities, and but for the master-stroke of the 10th of August, he and his satellites would probably have formed the van or the rear of the Prussians, and would have come with

them to the gates of Paris to destroy the factions !
In short, we should have been in counter-revolution, and the Constitution used for wadding in the
traitors' guns. *I do not exaggerate when I say it
would have rained blood.* Besides, we are not yet
out of danger, the combined work of three years of
treason keeps us on the brink of ruin ; only, fortunately for us patriots, we never lose courage or
hope.

Adhesions arrive at the Assembly from every side,
only the department of the two Sèvres, made
fanatical by the priests, has raised the standard of
rebellion.

As you see the *Moniteur* every day, I need not
tell you anything about the meetings of the Senate ;
I had rather keep you informed of our sayings and
doings. In spite of the first raid on the counter-
revolutionary printing-press, little aristocratic pam-
phlets sometimes appear, making their last desperate
efforts to corrupt public opinion.

The patrols are so numerous, and make such
repeated rounds, that it is like successive showers of
rain in this quarter, which is a very silent one, no
fortified town was ever better guarded. There are
the 50,000 men on foot, no longer .the National
Guard, but all the citizens dressed in every colour,
and armed with pikes for want of guns.

The Orleans tribunal has condemned a criminal
to death, a person of no note, with whose name I am
unacquainted. Some troops have been sent there

from Paris, lest the prisoners should attempt to escape. If our calculations are exact, those wretches of Prussians must be at Thionville, and the thought of the horrors they may perpetrate makes me shudder, for Merlin's father, who is administrator there, has written that the inhabitants are in no state of defence, but that they are resolved to bury themselves under the ruins of their town, rather than imitate Longwy.

Two o'clock, a.m.

I have just received a nocturnal visit from a dozen or so of brave fellows, of whom half-a-dozen came into the house. I presented the gun to them as a patriotic offering, and not as a capture, but they would not take it. The *commissaire*, whom I do not know, but who knows my patriotism, was extremely polite, and I responded to his politeness by an offer of refreshments, which was refused. I so strongly approve the measure and the vigilance of the people, that I could have cried *Bravo !* and *Vive la Nation !*

Thursday, August 30.

There have been several arrests, but I cannot get any details ; there is, however, no doubt but that the troops and the fortified places will make a vigorous resistance. Four camps are being formed around Paris, moats are being dug, and everything is being put in a state of defence.

Last night, all the silver vessels of the Sainte Chape which had been secreted by our enemies, were seized.   What a situation we are in, and how terribly the commonwealth is threatened, although it is so well defended !

Friday, August 31.

The discussions between the Senate and the Muncipality make us anxious, but we live in an atmosphere of storms, and are used to it.

Savoy has declared an armed neutrality; the peoples will not fight against each other.

LXV.

Paris, *August* 29, 1792.

The taking of Longwy has alarmed us and encouraged the aristocrats.   The effect of treason is as clear as day ; but that hideous monster exists everywhere, and can make us the victims of our ferocious enemies.   Servan immediately ordered the traitors to be punished.   But to whom has he given the order ?   To Luckner, and that while we are wondering to see the unmasked rogue still there !   In all this there is some confusion, and we shall have many a struggle to maintain before the victory is certain.   Twelve commissioners have been named, and sent to cashier all the bad officers in the army, and new measures have been taken for securing fresh levies of men, reinforcements of troops, and arms for the citizens.   The decree of accusation against Lajard, De Graves, and Martonne, is a tardy punishment for the false security which they inspired in us, and which has been the cause of all our disasters. I weep tears of blood over the private misfortunes which ravage our frontiers; and, in the traitors who are the authors of all our ills, I see only monsters and enemies of humanity who deserve a thousand deaths. The National Assembly and the Executive Council are in permanent activity, but they cannot undo with one touch of the wand the treacherous deeds of a bloodthirsty court, which, for three years, has been working our ruin, and weaving the web which envelopes us now. It is true we have broken through many of its meshes, but there still remain enough to cause terrible bloodshed.

I almost reproach Providence for not permitting me to be with you at this critical moment, and yet, for other reasons, I am glad of it, for when one is in so many difficulties, it is better to swim with the current, without any reference to the guidings of prudence, since in such unforeseen circumstances judgment is sure to be at fault.

Kersaint and his two colleagues returned to the Assembly yesterday. Their report was extremely interesting. The capital is tranquil, although in most active agitation. The enlistments, the nominations, the expeditions, and above all the *surveillance*, brings everything into action. Many people begin to see what you perceived on the night the Bastille was taken, and that causes them so to admire your insight into things, that by their desire your friends, except myself, are all conspiring against your peace. I remain passive on the subject.

R

The decree of the Assembly, summoning philosophers of all nations to the National French Convention, makes me hope that cowards and traitors
will not aspire to the honour of sullying it by their
presence. However, we are waiting for some very
great event; a little success for our armies would
be balm to the hearts of all the genuine friends of
liberty, and would give an advantageous impulse to
the vessel of the State, which is assailed by every
wind. I am waiting and hoping for it, for in our
present anxious position we hardly dare to breathe,
and yet I cannot help remarking again on the imposing calm of Paris, and the grand means of defence
which are being everywhere employed. Days seem
centuries to me ; I want news of you and Jules, for
I am alone with my boy, having no other guide
than my heart, and that makes me suffer, by
anticipation, all the consequences of the wrongs
which are plotted against us. Yesterday I saw the
two Messieurs Julliot; one of them has been on
guard at the Temple. It appears that Louis is
completely indifferent, and Médicis mingles with
her pride all the soft perfidies of her sex. Iron bars
have been put to their windows, but they are so
blind to their real situation that they told the
workman they should remain there too short a time
to render the expense necessary. The stupid
aristocrats are living in the same hope, they already
think they can see eighty thousand Prussians at
Paris dictating the bloody laws they, long for in

their own petty interests ; but though we have been deceived so many times our confidence remains unshaken. The leaven of discord between the Corps Législatif, the Department and the Muncipality, does not fail to ferment, and it makes us anxious. Troops have been sent to Orleans to reinforce the guard of the prisoners, and reinforcements have also been ordered for the frontiers. Camps are being prepared ; every available thing is being turned into guns and arms ; the attributes of royalty are being effaced wherever they are found ; and lastly, searches, that have brought quantities of arms to light, have been effected at the houses of the aristocracy. We must conquer or die, there is no middle course. Kersaint's report, which I have just read, makes me tremble. The nets were so well spread around us on every side that, but for the 10th of August, we should have been utterly lost. We are still on our guard, and it appears that the departure of certain commissioners has been suspended, for fear of depriving the Assembly of its warmest and most intelligent defenders. Andouin, Prudhomne, and other patriotic writers cry "to arms !" they sound the charge and the victory ; but all the same we shall be lost, if we do not save ourselves by prodigies of courage. Adhesions and gifts are poured in upon the National Assembly as if no Prussians existed. Money is reappearing a little, but it is only sold under the rose. The police are so vigilant that the day before yesterday

there were a dozen rogues put in the pillory, and
three men guillotined for fabricating false *assignats.*
You see our situation. I would write to you every
day if I were not afraid of sending you false news ; it
is necessary to wait for the confirmation of what
one hears, so as not to say foolish things that one
has to contradict in the next letter. Patriotic
courage is at such a height that nothing can equal
it, everybody's life is at stake, so you may imagine
the vigilance that is exercised. This makes people
particular, scrupulous and attentive as to the
nomination of the legislators who will hold in their
hands the last thread of the safety of the country.
I am ready to hide myself in terror when I think of
the danger and importance of their functions.

Be very prudent in communicating the contents
of my letters ; we must rouse up courage by every
means, it is our only chance of safety.

LXVI.

To her Husband.

Paris, *August* 30, 1792.

In two hours' time, yesterday, at about night-fall,
fifty thousand men were brought together, and all
the people were in the streets, which were illuminated
and traversed by patrols, making night as lively as
day. We could not have been more wide-awake if
the Prussians had been at the gates, but it was only
to have every house visited and searched for the

purpose of taking possession of all weapons not in use, or in bad hands. Large captures of guns belonging to aristocrats were made, in the execution of a measure induced by their mad ambition. The cowardice of Longwy has encouraged them, they cried victory! declared that the Prussians would be at the gates of Paris in a week, that they would prepare quarters for them, &c. Fortunately we are not yet arrived at that extremity, and we hope to frustrate their plans; camps are being formed, moats dug, arsenals ransacked, and every means of defence employed that such a calamity would demand. This is the work of traitors, and their accomplices the Feuillantin monarchists, an accursed brood, which has brought France to the brink of ruin. The enemy is before Thionville, and if we do not accomplish prodigies of valour to rouse our courage, utter despair will be all that is left to us. Those unworthy Frenchmen who prefer the Prussian law to liberty and equality, may find it cost them dear; for public opinion is strong and decided, adhesions are general, the constituted authorities are agreed on all points, and our only resource is "*to conquer or die.*" Try to impress that thoroughly on our Drômain and Romain brethren. The National Convention, if well composed, will prove our palladium; if badly, we are lost. Stringent measures are taken to keep suspicious characters out of it, but between this and then some decisive events will have taken place. What I consider as a special grace is the calm that reigns here; security is no sooner troubled than it is re-established; a hurricane over a serene sky, only covering it for a moment. This can only come from the consciousness of our strength, and I notice it after every shock, in the streets and public places, for it is there that public opinion shows itself. Aristocrats see the world through the prism of their passions, and think themselves all-powerful. That reminds me that your most humble servant had visitors last night after midnight. I produced your gun, which was the only weapon in the house, and offered it, but the opinion was that it should be left for the brave brother-in-arms who was on the point of returning, and might make a worthy use of it. There was an interchange of politeness, and I have come to the conclusion that whoever is afraid of such a visit as that, must be either very silly or very guilty. I asked them not to go to my old-lady-neighbour's, and on giving my word of honour, they passed her over. The *commissaire* had forgotten his umbrella, and came back to fetch it this morning, he told me he had taken four pistols loaded with ball, at Sareste's house. Sareste has reached Burgundy since the blessed 10th of August. Besides that, there was no other event of importance beyond the removal of the Eudistes, who were all refractory priests. During the perquisitions, all the plate belonging to the Sainte Chapelle was found hidden under a fountain. I can tell you nothing certain about the other quarters, they talk of cart-loads of

arms and cart-loads of aristocrats all deposited in
safe keeping. The operations are being carried on
to-day in perfect quiet, which has not necessitated
one call to arms. We are breathlessly waiting for
news of Thionville; we would give anything to gain
a victory. I have written to Jules, of whose final
resolution I am in ignorance; perhaps he is already
on the road. And you, my husband, what are you
doing? Where are you? How delightful it would
be to press you both to my heart! The Jacobin
emperor is my only resource in my solitude, everything is rose-colour to him, and he would sing *Ça ira*
under the very nose of the Prussians, he cannot
endure the least sign of fear, and is the optimist of
the Revolution. When I sometimes indulge in
alarming forebodings, he is as angry as if I had
doubted the Divinity. The prisoners of the Temple
contrive to carry on communications with the outside,
which oblige their keepers to use rigorous measures.
M. Julliot told me he had been present at the lessons
Médicis gives her son. She teaches him to recite,
before the guards, verses by I do not know whom,
which end thus :—

> "Et d'un peuple rebelle abhorrant le noirceur,
> Il faut, mon fils, apprendre à lui percer le cœur."

The application of this? I tell you these lines all
wrong very likely, and can only answer for the
sentiment of them. The guards of the château
are the best among our officers. She tries to win

them over, or to make them "suspected," and clearly she does not lose her time, for she is well informed of all that passes. Different stories are told of the means she employs, but I will not write rashly.

I have not gone to the National Assembly for an age. They are in a very critical state, and appear in general most cowardly, yet they enjoy entire confidence and can do anything they please. Luckner's nomination as generalissimo has stunned us all. Perhaps it is prudent to prevent his doing any harm here, and to keep him near us by an insignificant honour which compromises no one. I do not much like the notion myself, but I suppose eagles see better than moles, so I resign myself. Servan, who is one-sixth of a king, has plenty to do. If the Provincial Council of the executive could content everybody, it might be a kind of government that would secure us from the plague of royalty, provided it was renewed often enough to avoid corruption. The trial they are going to make might give them a taste for it, but that is a subject I do not consider myself capable of treating, so I merely touch on it in passing.

Thursday Morning.

I have just heard that the Senate dissolved the Municipality yesterday evening, and that the forty-eight sections re-established it during the night, and threatened the Senate. It is unfortunately true that there are bad citizens everywhere who spoil all, and this event alarms me. The results of it will

be known to-day. I ought not to tell you about it,
for when you read my letter we shall be reassured,
and you will have been disturbed for nothing. Say
not a word about it—it may blow over. There are
firebrands and worthless scamps in the Commune,
but their intrepidity produced the event of the 10th.
At that time, if we had only had quiet people on
our side, the counter-revolution would have been an
accomplished fact. It is best to purify by degrees,
and not to destroy all at once; and the Senate, on
their side, are far more corrupt than the Commune;
indeed, although regarded as a rallying-point and a
means of safety, they are not held in any great
admiration. Providence often employs the vilest
means for the noblest ends, and nature produces its
greatest beauties from the meanest sources; so
those who think of the commonwealth only, do not
regard individuals, but note in a general way all
that is good and all that is bad. I am anxious to
know what they will do to-day.

The neutrality of England has been strengthened
rather than weakened by the event of the 10th.
They say that Savoy has declared an armed neutrality. The Prussians are encamped at Fontoi and
threaten Thionville. We are in a terrible strait,
but the protecting angel of France watches over the
great destiny of the country, and victory is certain.

I fancy I recognized Jules' style in a long and
interesting note I read in the paper yesterday evening. It was dated from London, the 24th, and was

very much to the point. Good-bye, dear husband;
be easy, as we are, and do not expect impossibilities.
If you know anything of human nature, one must
look for storms and shocks when all the winds of
heaven are let loose.

I am going to the National Assembly to-day, and
shall not write again till the day after to-morrow.

There was an immense number of adhesions yesterday, and a superb report by Kersaint in the
Moniteur, in which La Fayette's crimes are distinctly
proved. If it had not been for the 10th, France
would have fallen back into slavery, and would have
beheld, despairing, its only chance of liberty drowned
in blood. Let no one judge unjustly of Paris; we
are doing wonders here, and I could tell you many
things, if you were here, that I cannot write. Has
Providence done well in not permitting me to go to
Dauphiny? That is a question that perhaps you
have decided for me. Adieu.

At four o'clock, I hear, the Commune has not
been re-established, but preliminaries are being
arranged. Fear nothing. Divorce is decreed, or
going to be. You have no longer a wife.

LXVII.

To her Husband.

Paris, *September* 1, 1792.

Good morning, my dear husband.—I begin the
month by saluting you, which is my method of

devotion. You must know that everything is going on as well as possible. Our friends, Pétion and Manuel, led the disgraced Municipality to the Senate yesterday, where they explained, were favourably listened to, had the honours of the sitting, and were applauded, so that affair is ended. The Municipality is vigorous enough to get the upper hand of the Senate; it is they who have the guard of the Temple, which is closely watched. They have issued a warrant against Dupré, who is Brissot's cat's-paw in the *Patriote Française*. All the Brissotin set is in despair because they have set aside the warrant by their own authority; but those little intrigues will not prevent the Great People from gaining their ends. The incorruptible Courbon insinuated on the platform that the Committee of Surveillance had saved the Prince de Poix and some others besides. Go on, my friend. Our legislature is ending as it began; but if you will give us a good National Convention, our future will be sure and brilliant. We want Roman courage and firmness.

It is generally reported that we have retaken Longwy, and made 6000 prisoners, amongst them the son of the King of Prussia. The news is not official, but I heard it whispered yesterday at the Assembly, and this morning I was told that during the evening it was universally rumoured at the palace (so-called) royal. Even though I should be obliged to contradict it, I must tell it to you;

besides I am certain we shall gain a victory soon, either this one or another. If you had heard Dumouriez's letter to Servan, yesterday, you would have cried " Bravo ! "

The elections are going on very well; quiet is undisturbed, though yesterday the acquittal of Montmorin roused the people a little, but the best thing is to let them alone, for if they were as indifferent as our unworthy representatives, and administered justice as badly, the counter-revolution would soon be triumphant, and great senators would speedily and readily bend the knee before tyranny. Let us say no more about them. I observed them closely yesterday, and their weakness made me so heart-sick that I shall not go there again for a fortnight.

I hope you admire your son's perfect submission. He is all hot-foot to come back. I have already signed the act of recall, and the poor child is only waiting for his father's approval to start. This is such a strong contrast to his Achilles-like character that I am quite touched by it. Write to him as quickly as possible.

Only let us have a good National Convention, and I prophesy liberty, peace, and every kind of prosperity, with an aureole of glory. Robespierre is at the head of the municipality, and Brissot directs the Senate. Can you see anything in that to quarrel about? Danton is as firm as a Roman; the executive council is good, and that is the cornerstone. The news of the taking of Longwy is confirmed; I have just been assured of it. How easily we believe what we wish ! The walls are placarded with so many suggestions for securing good deputies, that bad citizens will not dare to aspire to an election. Our section has excellent electors. Tallien spoke boldly before the National Assembly, and was supported by Manuel and Pétion; and *Ça ira, ça ira.* Adieu.

LXVIII.

To her Husband.

Paris, *September* 2, 1792.

"Who wishes the end, wishes the means." Let us have no barbarous humanity. The people have risen, and, terrible in their fury, avenge the crimes of three years of the most cowardly treachery. I should like to take refuge in your arms, my dear husband, to shed a flood of tears there, but first of all I must tell you France is saved! The tears I shed are for the unhappy fate of our brother patriots, fallen beneath the Prussian steel! Verdun is besieged, and cannot hold out two days. The joy of our ferocious aristocrats is a striking contrast to our profound affliction. We listened tremblingly to the alarm-gun which boomed out about mid-day. The tocsin sounded, the call to arms was beaten, people came and went in the streets, and everything was in the most violent agitation. The pathetic proclamations of the municipality attracted the attention of the people and touched their hearts: " Fly to the help of your brethren! " " To arms! to arms! " They hastened to obey, and to-night forty thousand men will march out, to fall upon the Prussians either at Verdun or nearer, if they advance. It is marvellous what a martial spirit possesses the Parisians—fathers of families, bourgeoisie, soldiers, *sans-culottes*—everybody is filled with it, and everybody is off to-night. The people think it is time to purge the earth of our enemies in the name of liberty, and not to leave their wives and children exposed in the midst of them. I must cast a veil over the crimes into which the people have been forced by those whose victims they have been for the last three years. The dark plots discovered on every side shed a frightful light, and an absolute certainty, on the fate which awaits the patriots. They must put to death, or be put to death! To what a horrible necessity does the fatal work of their enemies drive them—heads cut off! priests massacred! . . . . I cannot give you the details, although my reason tells me that kings and Prussians would have done a thousand times worse. If the people . . . . Ah! unhappy people, let us beware how we calumniate them!

Would you believe that I have been at the Tuileries from six o'clock until eight. A crowd everywhere, agitated, but cool and orderly. There is no more night at Paris, illuminations succeed to daylight. There are two magnificent pyramids of light at the great fountain, and the shops in the principal walks are lighted up. The Terrace of the Feuillants is as light as day, and full of groups of men, women, and children, all ready to follow the most generous or the most terrible purposes. Some of the deputies of the Assembly have just passed, escorted by troops; they are going to give the people peaceable advice. Seventeen persons, amongst whom they say were some deputies, were arrested at the barriers, and brought back to the Abbaye. An angry crowd broke open the gates at the back of the prison, and spared them the trouble of entering. This is terrible. I heard Cambon insinuating that the *Comité de surveillance* had released the Prince de Poix. Give us an incorruptible National Convention, or let cowardly Frenchmen fall into the Prussian nets. That would be no worse than having such base representatives. They did wonders this evening; I heard repeated bravos! If they succeeded in getting this Assembly to hold their sittings outside Paris, as some fools wish, Neros and Médicis would soon spring up again from their ashes. We took a carriage, for the disturbed state of the people and the darkness of the night filled me with secret terror. As we were getting in, a friend of M. de Sillery stopped me to tell me that noble patriot was arriving from Rheims to-night, choking with indignation. We have no arms, and are delivered up to the enemy bound hand and foot.

M. d'Orleans is an elector, and all our electors are good. The list of deputies whom the public calls to the National Convention has been made. It is the flower of France. If you had seen Paris as I saw it to-day, you would not have dared for one moment to doubt of the commonwealth. There was not a single Feuillant in the 300,000 men that I have seen disputing the honour of going to fight for their country; they were animated by a passionate courage and a perfect union. All the Feuillants are hidden in their cellars.

I got home at half-past eight, having observed the same movement, and the streets full of people from the Pointe Saint-Eustache up to this house; and I found our good friends Tiberge and Gabrielle; they had taken refuge with us because of the aristocratic tendencies of the house they live in. They slept in our bed. From them I heard that the people, in considerable numbers and in good order, were keeping a strict watch, and that some terrible things had taken place. The most perfect calm reigned last night, no noise of drums, nor bells, nor anything that generally precedes sinister events. My mind is so unsettled that I cannot sleep, and I have such a violent headache that I cannot continue writing. A thousand kind messages to the hospitable house you are in. I hold M. Blachette in such great esteem, that I form designs against his peace, and nominate him for the Convention. What we want is true patriots and true men. Offer my excuses and my compliments, dear husband, to the worthy wife of that courageous friend of liberty. I wish it was to-morrow.

We should be lost over and over again, if the Providence of the Revolution did not work fresh miracles every day. The tocsin ought to sound in every corner of France, and the departments to take example by the proud attitude of the capital, that they may not become the prey of our enemies. Nothing can save us but perfect unity. We have armies, National Guards, and a crowd of citizens who will surround the enemy. There are no more traitors at the head of our troops, and the victory is ours! But it must be a prompt one, or we shall have famine to fear, for there will be two hundred thousand men on the frontiers at one and the same time. Oh, my husband, what times we live in! Do not, however, be uneasy; though the Austrians and Prussians were at the gates of Paris, I would not make one backward step, but exclaim with more certainty than ever, "Victory is ours!"

Dismay and terror have seized hold of me; I know not what I feel. Six masons, who have just come from their work, have given the following details. A band of the people, struck by the imminent danger that would ensue if the malefactors of all the prisons fell upon us, in the event of a successful conspiracy, or the approach of the Prussians, have gone to each prison in succession accompanied by judges, and have massacred all the robbers, the

s

forgers, and the counter-revolutionaries; delivered the prisoners for debt, and taken those imprisoned for slight offences into their ranks. In this way they have emptied all the prisons, even Bicêtre, where they now are. The national gendarmerie and the other troops had said to the citizens, " Comrades, we leave our wives and children under your guard, protect them from the enemy at home, who might kill them while we are fighting the enemy abroad." It is said that these new executions of a terrible and wild justice were accomplished with remarkable coolness. Several priests were sacrificed to the popular vengeance. The masons who told me this, saw heaps of corpses at the prison doors. My profound humanity makes me weep over the fate of both the guilty and the innocent thus confounded. O God, have pity on a people who are driven to carnage. Do not impute to them . . . .

My mind is overwhelmed! Though the Prussians numbered a hundred thousand, they shall all perish, for the rage and horror excited by their unjust invasion is the secondary cause of these atrocious acts. With what furious zeal our brave volunteers left Paris! They are sure to die, or return victorious.

Adieu, dear husband. The masons, one of whom witnessed it all, related it to me with ingenuous simplicity, and sincere regret that the people should be forced to such extremes, and obliged to do justice themselves to escape from their enemies, the traitors and conspirators.

LXIX.

To her Husband.

PARIS, *September* 3, 1792.

MY DEAR HUSBAND,—Profound quiet is the result of this popular judgment, which was supported by the National Guard, and assisted by fifteen judges chosen in the crowd. A whole day was passed at Bicêtre. There is not a single living creature in any one of the prisons; some have perished, and the others have been set at liberty.

I must tell you that I am profoundly distressed and horrified at this terrible event. It is said that certain proofs of a great plot, in which all the criminals were to be the instruments of the crime, were discovered. Pétion did not answer for the safety of the capital after twelve o'clock last night, so we must believe that Providence has again miraculously saved us.

Here is a characteristic trait of the respect in which the people hold their representatives. Journeau, who has had a quarrel with Grangeneuve, was a prisoner at the Abbaye. A gunner was sent off to the Assembly to inquire if he was really a deputy, and on hearing that it was true, he was taken away with every attention that the dignity of his position called for; and yet he is a well-known aristocrat. Mesdames de Lamballe and Tourzel, who were at La Force, did not enjoy the same privilege, they are

s 2

amongst the victims; but the daughter of the latter, a child of twelve, and Madame Bithe, who is *enceinte*, were put under the care of the people, and faithfully protected.

It is reported that the enemy has been obliged to fall back on Longwy, which will soon be retaken. We have obtained a certain advantage, but the details are not very clear, and as I wish to give you only accurate news, I shall wait to be better informed. But as the hope is not without foundation, I want you to enjoy your share of it at once. Troops leave at stated intervals to facilitate the supply of provisions, and from the ardour they show a most brilliant victory is predicted. France is saved, but our brave brethren in the departments must imitate our devotion to the cause. The only interests at heart now are those of the country. The only feeling one has is love for the country; and, in short, its safety is our dearest wish, and absorbs every other thought.

I hear that the bloody tribunal is to be transported to Orleans. The Assembly have decreed the transfer of the prisoners to a fortified castle at Saumur. They simply mentioned in their official report the turn events have taken, and then resumed their labours.

The two Montmorins have shared the fate of the other criminals, and yesterday morning, the major of the Swiss Guard who had been judged by the tribunal of the palace, was guillotined; but it was the

people who immolated the two Montmorins. The
heaps of dead who were left in the courtyards of
the prison were taken in carts to Clamart. We have
not gone outside our door. Auguste and I are so
extremely sensitive that we dare not go out for fear
of meeting a dead-cart.

We have but one chance of safety, to conquer or
to die! The people are so convinced of the truth of
this, that they are all transformed into heroes, to
crush the Prussians, the Austrians, and all those who
want to devastate and enslave our France. The
same ardour that you noticed at the works at the
Champ de Mars, is displayed in the preparing of the
camps which are to surround Paris. Pétion and
Manuel continue to be the chosen magistrates of
the people. There have been some changes in the
municipality, but I do not know exactly what. I
was anxious to write to you this morning, because
at this terrible crisis it is a comfort to have direct
news of the state of the capital, and the lives of
those who are dear to one. We all feel that these
frightful events must be bringing us to the end of
our troubles, and securing the future of a great
people, who have been too long the tools of schemers
and conspirators. Perfect confidence is felt in the
Executive Power which governs us.

The elections are going on, and in the *Révolution
de Paris* you will see all the instructions given for
directing them, and the preachers have combined with
the defenders of liberty to disseminate them. There

was a sermon on Sunday which filled all Paris with admiration.

I know nobody, happily, amongst the unfortunate priests who were sacrificed.

No one is allowed to leave Paris, but I hope this crisis is drawing to an end, and that free circulation will soon be re-established.

LXX.

PARIS, *September* 6, 1792.

Patriotism triumphs, the enlistments and the departure of the enlisted give fresh life to the capital, and such an impulse to trade that the shop-keepers are bound to become patriots. Gaiety and safety march hand in hand to the sound of the drum. Federals are to be seen, and music is to be heard, everywhere. The streets are filled with the immense population which makes one think the whole universe must be in Paris, and every one cries *"Long live the Nation!"* We do not look like a threatened people, nor a defeated people, but like a large family enjoying themselves. Whoever has any other idea of the state of the capital, does not know the French. A veil is thrown over the hideous picture of late events, the discovery of the most infernal machinations does away with regret, for if the people had not purged the earth of the villains who were in the prisons, they would have saturated it with the blood of the people. Arms, money, and every proof of a most odious plot which was to have annihilated the patriots in the night of the 5th and 6th of September, have been found, and if Pétion and Manuel had not had some indications, things would not have been carried to so sad and frightful an extremity; but everything becomes lawful for just and necessary defence. Would you believe that our enemies are still conspiring ? hardly is one web broken than another is woven ; they are meditating a last and desperate blow, and expecting their dear Prussians.

A most inconceivable thing is that we get but vague news of the war. One half of Paris maintains that Verdun is taken, the other that the citadel still holds out, and the two generals do not say one word about it in their despatches to Servan, which were read to-day. Report says that Champagne and Burgundy have furnished more than 50,000 men, Paris alone has done as much. It is thought that our troops will surround the invading army on one side, while the new levies surround it on the other ; so that the Austrians and Prussians will be between two fires without any chance of escape. That will cause, I should think, such a terrible struggle, that before a week our fate, the fate of the nation, will be settled for ever. I am ill with anxiety, and I am so afraid of our armies being attacked by famine that I would rather they gained the victory by storm. Luckner is at Châlons. Pétion, Robespierre, Collot d'Herbois, Garan de

Coulon, Lacroix Albitte, Brissot, Thouret, Pastorel, Massieu, Calon, &c., are elected deputies to the National Convention for Paris and the neighbourhood. The tares are again mingled with the wheat, but in small quantities. Patience and courage! It is reported that Marat is named, but I will not believe it. The municipality is the same as on the 10th of August. Roland was denounced to it, and thereupon he wrote such a clever letter that the Commune itself must strike its colours. This leaven of discord has nothing alarming in it, it pushes us on to better things. The Senate seem torpid. They listen to splendid petitions, full of the fire of genius, and the love of liberty ; I heard some to-day that Demosthenes need not have disowned. Gold, silver, and *assignats* rain on the bureau ; in short, rivers may flow back to their sources, but we shall not perish. I do not know how to depict the generous ardour that fires our patriotic troops. I have no words in which to represent the surprising and animated spectacle the capital presents. I have gone to the Commune, the National Assembly, the Palace, and everywhere the calm and the agitation form such a grand contrast that I should like to be always in public places to admire it. Comrades, brethren, nothing is heard now but those sweet expressions, and all hearts are united and warmed by beneficent equality. The foolish Feuillantins, who are like children, believe the people are going to devour them, and as they have all conspired against

the people with their barbarous moderatism, and
are regarded with suspicion as signatories to the
petition against Pétion, they are afraid. C. and
B. are foolish enough to act like Dionysius the
tyrant. No one ever knows where they sleep. This
is the last insult they offer to the poor people, who
think very little about them.

Yet it is these dull instruments that despotism
made use of to attain its ends; and those who
regard the deeds of the people with horror, would
consider it quite natural and proper that 20,000
Jacobins should fall beneath the sword of the law,
wielded by a judge bribed by the civil list. They
would have said to their master, "By devouring
them, my lord, you did them much honour." As
for the judges, they have been guided by the constitution, and have obeyed the laws. The crime of
those rascals of Jacobins was to wish the world to be
governed by justice and reason, and the Rights of
Man to be no longer a dream. By the way, there
are no longer any Jacobins, the society is broken up
and now forms only a corporation. There exists
but one unity, the *French Republic*, and it was not
the Jacobins, but our enemies, who had the honour
of proclaiming it. If the course of events becomes
more tranquil, as our excellent mayor declares to-
day it will, I shall not use my pen so much; my
masons give me every morning the bulletin of the
preceding night. One of them has seen everything,
without taking any share in the sanguinary deeds

that have been done, for he possesses both humanity
and good sense.   If I were to calculate what those
cruelties are worth to us, by the proof he furnishes
me, I should say there was a difference of one to 1000
in the number of the victims, and in the selection,
that of an individual condemned to be hanged for
murder, or forgery, instead of Pétion, Robespierre,
Dubois de Crancé, Manuel, you, I, our children, and
all those who profess the sound maxims of justice,
philosophy, and humanity.

The tranquillity of Paris is so perfectly established
that the gates are reopened.   All the timid ones of
the four parties will get away as fast as they can,
but I shall remain at my post, until I know what
you and our son mean to do.   The cowardice and
selfishness of those who attack us have made me
intrepid, and yet for the last week I have neither
eaten nor slept, but have been in a state of mortal
anxiety.

The conspirators were bribed from the civil list;
the proofs of this are convincing even to fools ; but
we had guessed it long ago.   There are many
deputies on the list whose names I will not mention,
but the people know them ; however, they have
nothing to fear for the moment, all infamous as
they are, for the respect of the people for the
National Assembly is carried to idolatry.

LXXI.

PARIS, *October* 17, 1792.

The question of armed force, which was being discussed when you left the Convention, has, I think, come to nothing. There is such a decided opinion on that subject, that if any one had the daring to remind the Assembly of it, he would be hissed into silence.

The Brissotins have got the upper hand. It is hopefully expected that a mass of men will rise, perfectly pure in intention, and, setting aside all party spirit, will go straight to the point. Dumouriez was very well received *à la française* by the Convention; but at the Jacobin club the reception was of a more manly and Republican kind. Collot d'Herbois infused some admonition into his praise; his speech was a pleasure to all free Frenchmen. The general replied like a Roman, and from thence he went, like a French fop, to show himself at the theatre, and be applauded. There is still a good deal of the old Adam amongst these new men. Dumouriez had better go and take up his winter quarters at Brussels, if he wants to be forgiven for appearing at Paris in spite of the decree.

Your father was at the tribune for half an hour, contending for his right to speak, which President Lacroix obstinately refused him. He wished, in the general's presence, to remind him of his guilty neglect of the law, and add a well-deserved reproach to the extravagant praises he had just received. This one trait of Republicanism would have restored the Assembly to favour, for the sickening incense they have lavished on the general has not been approved. On the following day your father sharply reprimanded the President before he took his seat, so that he filled his post rather less tyrannically. I tell you this merely to show you what difficulties there are in the laborious functions of a legislator.

I have not gone to the Assembly since your departure. Your papa, whom I see every evening, seems less dissatisfied with it, though many of its members are very dull and vapid. Our Parisian deputation does not dare to whisper a word, but when the clouds of prejudice are dispersed it will show itself. It will be a surprise when Danton, Robespierre, and others, whom I will not name out of consideration for the weakness of human nature, appear as the strong pillars of liberty, and the sincerest Republicans.

You will see by the bulletin that the success of our arms surpasses all our hopes. There is some talk of declaring war with Spain, who is preparing for it secretly and treacherously. You will find the army afoot when you arrive. I mean our army, for they say that all in the neighbourhood of the Pyrenees are ready to take up arms and march against the enemy. Quantities of clothes are being made here for the soldiers, all the tailors are at work upon them. The camp will be abandoned, and the workmen scattered, of which I am glad, for evil-minded persons were not wanting amongst them to mislead the people. All the calumnies that were circulated about the Parisian gendarmerie and the different Parisian battalions, were for the purpose of having the guard armed. When truth shines forth, crime disappears. Seek and follow out the threads of that intrigue in the good newspapers.

LXXII.

I am going to talk politics, and yet I shrink from the bare idea of it. I see a Republic without Republicans, and I feel that I shall only find one that comes up to my notions in the future generation, which, as yet, is but budding and sprouting; still I flatter myself it will develope the virtues I am hoping for. Between this time and that, my dear son, how much must those who, like ourselves, have risen to the height which the revolution had reached at its first check, by the love of humanity and the hope of ameliorating the fate of man, suffer from the general corruption which is the present obstacle to everything ! There are already so many changes in our manners and opinions, that good and evil are unsuccessfully counterbalanced. Camille Desmoulins' journal, which I sent to your uncle Henry yesterday, as well as the other papers you will pick up on your way, will give you all the

details you ask for respecting the National Convention. I can tell you nothing, for I have not gone there
twice during your absence, and I have persuaded
the citizeness Lavit, who is more clever than I in
accomplishing the task she has set herself, to inform
you of everything. Your father, who enjoys good
health, fills his post of legislator philosophically.
He observes everything, and despairs of nothing.
He has spoken twice in the midst of an uproar,
although his intentions and the things he said were
both equally excellent. He pleads the cause of
poverty against the order of the day on the paper
money with which Paris is deluged, and also against
a diatribe concerning the deputation of Paris. The
friends of justice and liberty are afflicted at the
artifices and intrigues of the Brissotins, which are
encouraged and propagated by Gorsas and the
Patriote Français. Do not be taken in by them.
As for me, I am persuaded that the tact and delicacy
of my sex, added to my four years of observation,
have put into my hands the touchstone of patriotism.
I have applied it to Brissot, Buzot, Guadet, &c.
*" How has such pure gold been changed into such base
metal ? "* Robespierre, Panis, Robert, stand the
test, and leave behind them marks of the finest
gold, in spite of their detractors.

My opinion is that the former want a Republic for
themselves and for the rich, and the latter want it
to be entirely popular and for the poor. This,
together with human passions, are the causes of the

scandalous dissensions in the senate. For the rest, the Brissotins make all the noise themselves; the others, as yet, do not dare to speak, thanks to the Medusa's head which the clever ones hold up to keep fools and imbeciles in check. Our Commune, which was so astutely calumniated, has just sent in most satisfactory accounts. Paris, the Commune, and the Deputation are in disgrace, principally because of the 2nd September, over which I cast a funeral veil watered by my tears. But that is another atrocity of their enemies. That bloody day saved the patriots from a new St. Bartholomew, and many who condemn it would have been amongst its first victims. All the political circumstances which surrounded us then are effaced from shallow minds. My son, the fable of the rabbits is the true history of man.

The provinces have only the roses of the Revolution, we have all the thorns and all the dangers. They hide from our brethren in the departments the generous devotion of the Parisians, and the sublime elevation of their views. The pigmies who ask the giants to guard them deceive them in everything.[1] This armed guard is the hope of the Lilliputians, but those who are really men wish for only two sentinels at the door of the Senate: love and justice.

I believe it will be decreed to-day that the

[1] The party of Brissot and the Gironde wanted at that time to decree the organization of a force from the departments, to guard the National Convention.

country is out of danger. There are no more slaves on the soil of liberty.

Dumouriez has gone. I am waiting to hear of his arrival at Brussels to forgive him. Anselme seems to me a republican, but then no reputation holds for very long, and we change as the men do.

LXXIII.

From M. J.

PARIS, *December* 15, 1792.
(First year of the Republic.)

I have received your letter and your speech; I am much pleased with them both. The mayor, Blachette, who wrote to me a few days ago, spoke very well of my son, but no one will ever speak so well as I think of him. You have a noble soul, excellent principles, strength of mind, talent, knowledge, and great facility and love for work. That is more than you need to make yourself a name, especially in the new state of things in which we live; but, my dear son, I am too anxious for your happiness to desire celebrity for you. I believe one never obtains that without paying dearly for it. You will tell me that you wish to acquire glory by none but virtuous means. I know it well, my dear child, but private virtues are sufficient for moral welfare, and are the most certain foundations of happiness. I am convinced of that by my own experience, which I could wish were not entirely lost for you. Your eagerness to make proselytes to the system of equality is doubtless very praiseworthy, but it will lead you astray if you cannot moderate it. Often, when working too zealously for the good of humanity, one only brings about one's own ruin. One should thoroughly know the men of one's time, and not try to transform the slaves of Cæsar into Catos. Our contemporaries are deeply corrupted, and I doubt very much if they will ever be true republicans. That end must be worked for, however, but with a wise circumspection. Never put yourself too forward, measure the strength of prejudices before you combat them, and only attack them indirectly unless you are sure of a complete victory. The great vice of our social state (and it is perhaps irremediable) comes from the monstrous inequality of fortune. The rich know perfectly well that such a state of things cannot exist long in a democratic republic, and that is what arouses their selfish ire so violently against a system of government which must, sooner or later, deprive them of a part of their fortune. They cannot conceal the fact that the poor and laborious classes, being the most numerous, must have a large share in the exercise of sovereignty, and that they will employ it to ameliorate their condition. If those who possess more than is necessary, were just and good, they would hasten to make some sacrifices in favour of their less fortunate brethren, and would by that means prevent many misfortunes. This is the

T

stumbling-block of modern philosophy. It has clearly established the equality of rights, but it wants to maintain that prodigious inequality of fortune which places the poor at the mercy of the rich, and renders the latter arbiter of all his rights, since he can deprive him of the right to exist. If this goes on, tyranny will revive. It is absolutely necessary, for the maintenance of the Republic, that the poorer citizens be assured of living in comfort on the proceeds of their toil, and that those who cannot work be fed and maintained at the expense of the public funds. Oh, my son, what troubles we must yet go through before we attain this end! All those who would be the protectors of the poor, will have the rich for their mortal enemies, and will run great risks of becoming their victims, for the rich have this advantage, that they can arm the indigent masses against themselves, by making them the assassins of their most ardent defenders. All that is required for that, is to monopolize the corn and cry out against the agitators. I myself, my dear son, am detested at this moment by the unhappy peasants of my canton, who have been persuaded that I moved in the National Convention to have all the mulberry-trees uprooted. The wicked will go to any excess, and the ignorant multitude believes everything.

The truth is that there never was a question of the mulberry-trees in the Convention. All you say will not prevent my always regretting my precious obscurity, and if you had as much wisdom as you have virtue, you would have urged me never to leave it. At fifty, one cannot change one's character, and a man who has kept himself up to that age apart from public business, and who feels equal repugnance and incapacity for it, should continue to hold himself aloof from it. I do not say this to you as a reproach, but to teach you never to put your own reason against that of a man whom experience has made sufficiently acquainted with himself and others to make him know better than any one else what is best for him to do. The Brissot faction does not dare to justify the king, but it is evidently trying to save him. Every day it checks the movements of the Convention by denunciations or incidents which upset the order of the Assembly, and cause the most scandalous scenes to take place. I do not know how it will all end, but we are surrounded by dangers, and do nothing to gain the confidence and love of the people, in which alone our safety consists. Adieu, my dear son, be faithful to your principles, but let the chief one be to act prudently, and not to advance too precipitately on an undermined soil. Sound the minds and hearts of men, before you allow full swing to your ideas and sentiments.

LXXIV.

PARIS, *December* 24, 1792.

Your papa, and all the patriots of the National

Convention are much dissatisfied. It is pitiable. The majority consists of fools and schemers. I think the Brissotins must be possessed. Roland has succeeded in corrupting public opinion in the departments, by bribing some of the patriotic journalists. Every day he takes two thousand numbers of Gorsas' paper. Those men, Gorsas, Brissot, Carra, spread clouds and darkness where formerly they caused light to shine. Their authority is so firmly established by three years of civic spirit, that one cannot believe in this horrid change without seeing to the bottom of the matter. Desmoulins and Merlin have been obliged to give up their journal, for want of subscribers. It seems that men only run after lies and errors, austere virtue has but a very small number of friends, she frightens some, she displeases others, and her court, which admits neither flatterers nor flatteries, is more deserted than that of her cowardly antagonist.

I would as soon live in the fields and forests as in the present state of society. It seems to me that the inhabitants of those places are less ferocious than our politicians, Brissotins, Girondins, &c. The revolution is rousing passions to such a white heat that men are becoming incomprehensible. How I invoke prudence to save you from the snares of the wicked! how I implore you to keep a seal on your lips, and not to let one word escape that might give a hold on you! You have the impetuosity not only of youth, but of your disposition; try to keep all this impetuosity so carefully shut up and fastened down that none of it may escape and betray you. A man's greatest merit and dignity consist in his empire over himself. Nothing is so foolish and weak as to give our enemies great advantages by our little failings, which nevertheless leave the soul and the heart pure, and only spoil, so to speak, the outside. The wicked know so well how to catch the well-intentioned in that trap. They make a crime of the least trifle, they turn about and about until they have entangled their prey in their nets. I tremble from head to foot, dear child, when I reflect on the dangers which threaten your youthful frankness, and the noble vigour of your mind. I recommend you to your own wisdom and your own watching. Your father was particularly pleased with the style of your letters, and above all with your principles. He has such confidence in you that it calms my anxiety and my maternal solicitude. He thinks you have sufficient prudence and moderation to steer your bark aright in spite of your natural vivacity. I am always picturing that precious little craft between Scylla and Charybdis. Your speechifying amongst the Jacobins of Toulouse made my flesh creep. I am afraid you will make yourself enemies ; but then I am a woman and a mother, so all this is natural, I do not pretend to be anything else.

LXXV.

PARIS, *December* 28, 1792.

I am sad at heart for the tempests which gather over our heads during these disastrous days. Before entering on my subject, I must tell you that as fast as my body gets well my mind falls sick. The apathy and enforced selfishness into which my sufferings threw me, were a double rampart against my sensibility. Now I feel that it is awaking once more, and I doubt whether I have gained by the change; for I am consumed by civic anxieties and solicitude, and that is a certain proof of health.

I recommend you, not to Fortune, not to Glory, not to the coarse god Plutus, but to the goddess Minerva—to holy virtue. The more those two divinities are neglected by the foolish, the more they are courted by the wise. They alone, my dear child, are worthy of your incense. The actual corruption of the age, and especially at the present time, must be a sovereign preservative for a noble soul. The contempt we feel for the conduct of such and such persons, is like a mirror which shows us how hideous we should be if we resembled them. We ought to keep such a mirror constantly before us, and scrupulously examine whether there be anything in ourselves which places us on a parallel with the persons whom it reflects. Be severe and formidable to yourself. Take council with your conscience and judge yourself *in petto*. Admit into this council, between your conscience and your heart, your two best friends, and consult them in imagination. Be good and virtuous, my child, I ask no more.

The National Convention is more agitated than the ocean in its wildest rage. One cannot bet for or against. The majority, seduced by the artifices of the Brissotins and the Rolandists, has been the tool of that cabal for the last three months. The true patriots, immovable in principle, and strong in their consciences, are so firm and active, that I still see victory hovering over them. Unfortunately they agree together like the builders of the Tower of Babel. It was a clever trick to make believe that they had a party and leaders, for that has isolated them, and made them keep themselves apart with scrupulous delicacy, while the enemy coalesced, assembled, and drew closer together, securing all the foolish people by the terror they have breathed over Paris. Your father has watched it all with the lynx eye of the philosopher, and a perfectly judicious mind.

Manuel is a turncoat. See what men are when they have neither morals nor faith! They give themselves to God or to the Devil, according to the interests of the moment; that is why I maintain that faith is as necessary to the vitality of the soul as water and fire are to the well-being of the body. But observe, with me, that there is no virtue without strength of mind, and that the most virtuous are corrupted if they associate with the wicked.

The worthy Pétion wears no longer the nuptial robe. His natural goodness and his kindnesses to men whom he thought virtuous have made him the tool of the cabal. I, who held him in tender veneration, and who am not easily to be detached from my friends, regard him as a dupe, but, if he persists, I shall consider him a bad patriot. He has already made more than one false step, and to be as indulgent as one is towards him requires the remembrance of all his former popularity.

Vergniaud, Gensonné, and Brissot are nowhere. No one would think they belonged to the Convention, but it is said they are working underground like moles—who are blind.

Saturday Morning.

Yesterday Robespierre made a speech on the necessity of judging and punishing the tyrant. He was heard in profound silence. Buzot, Rabant, Saint Etienne spoke after him, but drily; they contended that an appeal should be made to the people; this would open the doors to civil war. We shall see to-day.

Best love to Saint Cyr. Is he pleased with his new functions, and what do you think of them, my dear child? I wish you every satisfaction, and if you do not find it where you are, I would advise you to seek it elsewhere. Your place procures you, to a certain extent, the means of exercising justice and benevolence; it pleases me for that reason, but be on your guard against sensibility, which ought always to be controlled by the strictest integrity. Remember also what is the basis of our new Government—equality and liberty. The meanest soldier is a man like the general. The only difference between them is that the soldier, being nearer nature, is probably better and less corrupt.

LXXVI.

PARIS, *January* 3, 1793.
(First year of the Republic.)

MY DEAR SON,—This is the opinion of . . . . disseminate it prudently. It is a question of attaching ourselves to things and not to men. If so-and-so speaks truth, of what importance are his name and prejudices? It is truth that we love and seek; so be it.

Paris is calm and the National Convention is perfectly dignified for the three last days. They neither approve nor disapprove. What a good thing it would be if the senators were gods! * * * *

LXXVII.

PARIS, *January* 5, 1793.
(First year of the Republic.)

The Rolandist faction gains the day in the Convention, and the volcanic eruptions of the mountain only produce a harmless noise. The Girondists are incredibly wicked. It is as clear as day that they

want to create disturbances, and if they do not wish
them to degenerate into civil war, they may some
day deplore the bloody dissensions they have excited.
Yesterday they asked and obtained that an infamous
diatribe against Paris, should be printed and sent to
all the departments. To-day our municipality has
presented a picture of our political and moral situation which is well calculated to dissipate the prejudices against us that calumnious productions have
excited in all the departments, whither it was just
and natural to send this counter-poison. Guadet
opposed it, speaking with the utmost bitterness
against the patriots, and on his motion three-fourths
of the Assembly decreed to pass to the order of the
day. The faction has not given up the project of
filling the *ci-devant* capital with departmental troops,
of producing a sort of partial insurrection, and of
taking advantage of it to drive out the Convention
from its midst. That intention is so manifest that
one must be blind not to see it.

My desire will always be that the laws may be
executed, however bad they may be, until they are
legally repealed.

Adieu, my dear son, I love you most tenderly,
and in confiding you to your own prudence, I de-
posit in your hands everything that is dearest and
most precious to me. Apply yourself to the study
of men, learn to appreciate them with a just severity,
and not to yield too easily to the sentiments of compassion and generosity you may feel for their mis-

fortunes, for it often happens that they have brought them on themselves by their own faults and vices.

LXXVIII.

PARIS, *January* 7, 1793.

I rejoiced my heart with that little sentence, " *I am well and happy.*" A thousand thanks to you, my son, for the care you take to spare your mother's sensibility. Those words in your postscript were a trait of delicate feeling that I appreciate all the more because I depend on your veracity. That is the foundation of all my joy and tranquillity. You must never seek to soothe me with flattering delusions. Truth will out, though at a thousand leagues of distance, and then all confidence is lost, and all security with it. To obtain any satisfaction in this world one must do one's duty, keep the soul healthy, the heart pure, and the mind upright. Take immense care of yourself, so as to enjoy those two treasures, health of body and health of mind. I am anxious to know whether you are overwhelmed with the weight of your burden; if so, you must lay it down. We leave you entirely to your own prudence and courage, yet I know by experience that at your age people presume too much on their strength, and often abuse it. Be careful, and remember that if you want to be a vigorous athlete, you must not begin by fighting with giants. Hercules strangled snakes before he slew lions. Above all, dear child, take care of my son, and watch over your most excellent father's dearest friend. You cannot imagine how dear you are to him, one little proof of this is his impatience while expecting your letters and his anxiety to send you news of us; he even surpasses me in that.

The election of Bournonville has given satisfaction, he is not at all Brissotin, and the Montagnards have all the glory of his elevation. If the odious faction had succeeded in placing there Achille du Châtelet, whom they had proposed, they would have regained all their fatal preponderance. The best of it is that they declare Pache will be a substitute, a general, or a simple volunteer; it is all the same to noble minds, provided they can find means to do good. I press you to my heart, and so good-bye.

LXXIX.

PARIS, *January* 8.
(First year of the Republic.)

Yesterday the debate on the great trial was adjourned until Monday, when it is to be terminated. There is so little appearance of unanimity in the Convention, that it will be a toss-up for or against. The majority seems to incline to the appeal to the people, but I have a feeling that the result will deceive the wisest, and that Providence will yet work one of those miracles which give free course to justice and frustrate all traitors. In the meantime, human prudence counts and calculates, and all are in suspense and anxiety.

If we could be made republicans by virtue of a decree, in the same way as we were given a republic, there would not be the least risk. Everything would be done with all the rigour of justice and of the laws, and that would turn our worst enemies into partisans of our side, for I have never yet seen them mastered by anything but fear.

From my observations amongst my acquaintances, I have come to the conclusion that all the aristocrats are Brissotins. You will see the *Révolution de Paris* this week. That paper has always been indulgent to the weaknesses of the faction, even when it attacked them, forced to it by the strength of truth. Barère blows hot and cold. I think he would like to keep in with both parties, so as to avoid shipwreck in case of a storm. Our brave Parisians are calm and tranquil, though the departments incessantly calumniate and threaten them. I wish they could all be in Paris, and see things as we see them, they would soon be enlightened, and would encourage us instead of fighting against us. I advise you, my dear child, always to be prudent and reserved, especially in public. I am not without anxieties about the dangers of the career upon which you have entered. Be master of yourself. I repeat that word to you over and over again, for it contains a book full of wisdom.

Do you often see Servan? If the brave general

will receive the expression of our esteem and gratitude, present it to him from us. Tell me about his son, I am greatly interested in him; I knew his mother, who was as full of merit as a woman could be, and her child must have inherited something of that, not to mention his taking after his father as well.

Be careful of your health, dear child, you must not take advantage of it because you are young. I like your patriotism, and I am always touched to tears at the good-will it procures you. Be prudent with everybody. Be indulgent and benevolent, and above all love justice, it is the queen of virtue. Be yourself in everything. Like the mother of Epaminondas, my greatest joy will be in the virtues of my son. Be on your guard against the delusions of self-love; as for a noble pride, it is the companion of an elevated mind.

In the midst of my rheumatic pains your letter made me shed tears of joy. I think it quite natural that you should find friends and admirers in all those who love what is good, and are enthusiastic about all that is beautiful. But the wicked will hate you for the same reasons that make the good love you. The fear of their hatred, or even of their fury, must not cause you to turn from the path of virtue, but it should induce you to walk in it with caution.

I do not know why I should give you advice when, from your conduct, I feel that I should do better to ask advice of you. Continue, dear child, to behave with the same wisdom and modesty. Be always master of yourself, that is the surest means of gaining the mastery over others, and do not always take advantage of your facility in speaking, but sometimes put off to another occasion the clever things you might have to say. In that way you will not wear out the admiration of your friends, nor change it into envy.

Robespierre's letters to Pétion are masterpieces of irony, but a style in which wit shines at the expense of good feeling never pleases me. Sometimes it is necessary to crush one's adversary, but that cannot be done lightly by any one with a feeling heart. Besides, Pétion is far from being contemptible, and if Robespierre had shown less disdain for him, he would have given proof of greater self-respect.

Adieu, my son. I suffer a great deal, and have not courage to write any more. I do not know what paper to send you. Louvet is on the *Débats* and the *Décrets*. The *Moniteur* presents the Brissotins under a deceitful and favourable aspect.

LXXX.

Paris, *January* 14, 1793.

You are entering upon a glorious but difficult career, my dear son. May heaven protect your steps, and preserve you in integrity and virtue! Your papa and I did not read your letter yesterday with dry eyes. My heart was at once oppressed and dilated with joy, while the natural nervousness of a woman showed me at a glance the dangers that accompany glory. Your papa, who is quite satisfied that you possess firm principles and a clear head, added to strength of mind which will ensure you all the courage you will need in every event, is unreservedly happy. He answers for your prudence and wisdom, and has no doubts of you in any way. What I esteem most in the world is the good-will of the people, because I really love them with all my heart. My interest in that suffering portion of society has always been excited by their misfortunes, and often increased by their virtues. But you know my opinion on that subject—but, what a responsibility for one so young! It will raise up enemies, perhaps persecutors for you, but that will only be a stimulant to the practice of virtue.

My dear boy, you must say to yourself, "There are those who watch all my steps, that they may catch me tripping; my least words, my most insignificant acts are noted by envious eyes." Now is the moment when that vigilant sentinel, your reason, must weigh and control your movements. You are so young to be left without guide or compass in a corrupt and corrupting world; but try to preserve the loving confidence of youth in your heart, the innocence of truth on your lips, and that love of your fellow-creatures which emanates from a really good heart. Strive to preserve that. Do not let flattery intoxicate you, nor little reverses discourage you ; walk firmly, obey your conscience, and take no pleasure in the praises of men, unless they are merited by the sternest virtue. Above all, be modest, that your fellows may not only support you, but love and esteem you, and try to conceal in a measure the superiority that nature has given you over some amongst them.

The article in Robespierre's paper, in which he so skilfully attacks and defeats Pétion, has caused me great pain. If Robespierre had been my husband or my son, I should have knelt at his feet, to induce him to forego that moment of revenge. No mean sentiments should have a place in a great soul. A grave and serious explanation will often turn and reunite upright minds, but sarcasm and ridicule are arms which inflict mortal wounds and produce deadly enmities. If you wish to be spared, spare others. I am so fondly anxious on your account that I should like to infuse all the virtues and all the wisdom of the Greeks and Romans into you, so that you might be all I wish. French virtues have not yet any republican strength ; we are degraded by ambition, intrigue, and the ignoble love of money.

I have nothing to tell you of the National Convention, except that it is crushed beneath a weight of ignominy. So much talent and so much vice never before met together for the shame and misfortune of humanity. Your papa, who went there

U

with a soul as pure as heaven, is amongst the Spartans of the Mountain, or rather the Three Hundred of Thermopyle.   There are about twenty more men like him, upright in intention, and sincerely republican, for which reason they are called seditious. They have to fight to be heard, when they want to speak the tribune is closed to them, and the Presidents are always ill-disposed and insolent beyond all bounds.

Our political horizon is dark with clouds.   We are all deeply concerned at the turn given to affairs by the spirit of faction.   Paris is continually threatened with the departments, but if they could be in the midst of their Parisian brethren, they would see and act as we do.   Do you want to know what the treacherous leaders would like to do ?   I can tell you, for I know it as well as if I was in the conspiracy.   They are trying to save the *ci-devant* king, remove the Convention from Paris, and make a Constitution according to their own ideas and favourable to the rich ; and if civil war is added next spring to the war with foreign powers, our schemers will only be all the more important, and all the more necessary.

Poor humanity !   Poor people !   Your father is so sad, so painfully distressed, that his depression adds to our troubles, and makes us still more unhappy.

Write to us often, our only consolation comes from you.   Be brief with your other correspondents, so as to have more time to give us. You write too much, and you sit up too late. I wish I could come to the door of your room as I used to do here, and persuade you to put out the hateful candle that keeps sleep from your eyes. Take care of your eyes, your health, your head, they all wear out like a coat, if you do not keep them in good order.

Do not speak so often at the club, my dear boy, lest you should wear out the public liking for budding talents, and also lest you should excite envy.

The departments are not as blind as Roland thinks they are, and as he would like them to be. They have sent him back from Arras great sealed up parcels of diatribes against the patriots. The faction is expecting some federals whom the departments are sending without any requisition, and in spite of the law; no doubt this is done to arouse some disturbance in Paris. But God guards us, and so we are well guarded.

LXXXI.

PARIS, *January* 20.
(First year of the Republic.)

Your father came home last night at three o'clock. The reprieve has been refused, and the decree ordains that the execution shall take place within twenty-four hours. The form and conduct of it are committed to the executive power. Public opinion is so strong and so pronounced, so powerful and so sovereign, that Paris remains majestically calm ; not a remonstrance or complaint is to be heard.

LXXXII.

PARIS, *January* 26.
(First year of the Republic.)

I had intended to devote the day to you, my dear son, but our good Mademoiselle Canot came to pass it with me. If I have not talked *to* you, I have talked a great deal *of* you ; you are always uppermost in my thoughts, and always the most agreeable subject of my discourse. I was neither astonished nor surprised at the event which has removed you from Toulouse ; it grieved me for a moment, and then my courage returned.

You have applied my favourite maxim, "Coolness and intrepidity vanquish all difficulties." You behaved with great wisdom, go on as you have begun ; above all, observe the greatest reserve in speaking of the generals who have behaved like children, in taking this petty vengeance, and have given a child the opportunity of showing himself more a man than they. Your answers seem to me laconic, measured and prudent. They are worthy of a Spartan.

I pity the ignoble means which those who are the slaves of their passions employ to gain their ends. They *must* bend and crawl, and I notice a certain deceitful cunning in the conduct of your two superiors, which makes me think that neither their hearts nor their consciences approve the energetic measures they require of you. They thought to ruin you, but in reality they have contributed to your reputation and glory, because your love of work and duty will make you equal to your new functions. That is the advice of a mother or a friend. If your health and happiness suffer by this new sort of life, there is still an honourable means of leaving it. Every public functionary should leave his place when he can no longer fill it properly. Youth and inexperience would be sufficient excuse for you. It is always noble and great to lay down a burden one can no longer bear, and we should always measure our strength prudently so as to undertake nothing beyond it, because that would give too great an advantage to our enemies, who would immediately accuse us of inordinate presumption. Your father says, that with the firmness of your character, and your zeal for the public welfare, you will succeed in everything, and this reassures me. Think of the country, of the public welfare, and leave personal interest and all the miserable little passions which agitate others a hundred leagues beneath you.

I feel an immense pity for the human species when I consider the civilized portion of it, and those who used to be called " *the great ;*" but I am comforted and consoled when I turn my eyes on the people. I have always observed amongst them that uprightness and native virtue which is far more worthy than regulated vice. This observation brings me into opposition with Robespierre, who says that virtue has always been in a minority in this world. Yes, because they who seek to govern are with those who are exposed to the strong light of day, and they who remain hidden in the crowd count for nothing.

The king's death passed off at Paris like the banishment of the Tarquins at Rome. The people displayed a majestic calm that would have done honour to the most palmy days of the Roman Republic. Our enemies, who stab from behind, like cowards as they are, threaten all the deputies who voted the death of their chief, so that I have my share of the alarm that they cause to those who take any interest in the matter. Your father is intrepid, and does not even think of it, but my heart is divided between you two, and I am in a constant state of anxiety. My ill-health, which continues, contributes not a little to encourage the phantoms of my imagination, so that my days pass sadly and drearily.

LXXXIII.

Paris, *January* 30.
(First year of the Republic.)

The great political events which have happened here have raised the public spirit, fired true republicans with a love of country worthy of Rome, and produced such perfect tranquillity in the capital that, for four years, it has not presented a quieter aspect. Truly there is a Providence which decrees; the Convention, united by the Divine Power that controls the world, merely sanctions. We laugh at the foreigners who want to go to war with us, they are less to be feared to-day than ever they were. They have no longer any supporters in France. Take care of yourself. After the health of the soul, that of the body is the greatest good. Adieu, dear child, I press you to my heart, and cover you with kisses; I can do no more, for pain stops my writing.

LXXXIV.

PARIS, *February* 1, 1793.

The Convention is sitting in permanence, and your father stays there night and day. Our sky begins to clear, but, so long as the storm lasted, Paris was in a state of effervescence, animated and valiant, but, at the same time, calm and orderly. The preponderance of strength in this great city, being that of the populace and public opinion, will always be the saving of the Republic. The infinite varieties blend, under circumstances of danger, into one firm and energetic purpose that carries all before it.

If infamous Brissotism had not been working at our alienation from the departments, no traitors would dare to show themselves openly. My belief is that Dumouriez's vast and black conspiracy was concerted with the leaders of that fatal party. Hundred-mouthed rumour declares it is so. The Don Quixote who tried to pass himself off as a little Cæsar, is fallen and swallowed up in the abyss he was digging beneath our feet. It is not yet known what his fate will be, whatever it may be it will not influence ours, and Heaven has manifested its anger against the wicked by the breath of its displeasure, which has dispersed their evil designs.

The Convention goes on pretty well, but public opinion is a thousand leagues above it and does so much to raise it to a higher level that hope begins to shine on every side. Bournonville was, some time ago, discovered to be his master's instrument; the mission he was charged with is regarded as a passport of emigration for him and a refuge against our just vengeance. Bouchette's election in his place, and Dampierre's in the place of Dumouriez, cause great public excitement. We are hoping at last to have leaders who are friends, after having had so many who were enemies. The antipathy of Dumouriez to Pache is now explained, and that excellent patriot's glory receives a new lustre from it, while our confidence in him as mayor has increased twofold. Our constituted authorities, departments, communes, municipalities, chiefs of the armed force, popular societies, and the majority of the sections, agree on the same points. It is not like the 10th of August when they were all in opposition.

The Convention, through the accursed faction which divides it, has been but a feeble rampart, and the Spartan deputies have had a hard struggle. I say nothing to you of those things which you can see in the papers, but, indeed, the labours of the Mountain, obliged to struggle against enemies inside and outside, are Herculean; and, when I hear your father telling all the evil they have done to produce good, I stand amazed at the blindness of the men assembled and their sacrilegious obstinacy. A dozen scoundrels who pull the wires suffice to cause the death of a multitude of human puppets who are their dupes until they become their victims.

Believe nothing of the Orleanist factions, nor of all the idle tales that are spread in the provinces. The son of *Egalité* [2] is implicated in the infamy of Dumouriez; that proves nothing except that the young man was ensnared by him. His father is allowed to come and go, but is always watched, but he is so antipathetic and held in so little esteem that this measure is taken solely for the satisfaction of those who are afraid of this phantom of a man.

LXXXV.

Paris, *February* 2, 1793.

Our political horizon has never been more serene, nor Paris ever more peaceful. The Convention is recovering itself, the Montagnards triumph, and

---

[2] The Duc de Chartres, afterwards King Louis Philippe.

attract so many from the Plain, that I do not doubt there will be a good majority when circumstances require it. You know, as well as I, that our occupation for the moment is the war with the Dutch and the English. It is not very alarming, and we have friends in the heart of the enemies' countries who might easily give their Cabinets some trouble.

The National Convention is organizing the Ministry of War. It is proposed to give six assistants to the Minister, and this proposal is well received because of the immense quantity of work there is to be done. It is thought Pache will be changed, his patriotism is not to the taste of everybody, and they fall back on his pretended want of intellect and capacity. The patriots, who like him much, will, at least, obtain a place for him as assistant-general. I go into no details on the articles decreed, you will find all that in the papers.

Robespierre and his brother and sister are to dine with us to-day. I shall thus make the acquaintance of that patriotic family, whose head has so many friends and so many enemies. I am curious to observe him closely. I should like Pache to keep his place because of his sincere patriotism. He has all my best wishes, but I feel *in petto* that they will not be granted.

Good-bye, dear child. Be patient and courageous in your new career ; may severe and inflexible virtue guide your steps. Our young men must bear in mind that we depend on their republican virtues for the safety and glory of the Republic. The elders will never be endowed with the spirit that suits the present state of things, they are too weak and corrupt. They have no strength of mind, no energy of thought, and new ideas cannot take root in old and muddy soil that has never produced anything but creeping plants.

LXXXVI.

PARIS, *February* 11, 1793.

If the French Executive Power, at that time composed of greybeards, had, last September, not only accepted but carried out the plan of a young man (a ten and a seven composed the age of the amiable youth), if, I say, the Executive Power had executed that well-devised system of enlightening the English people, George and Pitt would have wasted their time and money, and we should not have gone to war with the English. Do you remember the letter you addressed to Lebrun, and how highly everybody approved of it? And then the neglect of that cold patriot, the political indifference which led to those prudent measures being abandoned? Well, all that was Brissot's doing. . . . .

Your new place, my dear commissioner, is according to the strongest desires of my heart. You will be able to do much good and exercise many virtues in it, above all, justice towards the poor and the weak. You must adopt the reverse of the old policy. Then all consideration, all attentions, all justice was for the great; the small fry of humanity, who are the most often worthy, were looked upon as inferior beings, who were undeserving of the attention of a man in authority. In these times, on the contrary, in your post, the soldier should possess your heart's best affections, your whole care and attention should be to preserve him from the habitual oppression of which he is the victim. Justice for all, especially for the poor and weak! Their most urgent needs are dependent on it, whereas the others can wait, being in the enjoyment of so many advantages, that what they ask for is often · only a superfluity of felicity. Justice and benevolence, these two are all the law and the prophets. I was much pleased with the Robespierre family.[3] The sister is *naïve* and natural like your aunts; she arrived two hours before her brother, and we chatted like two old women. I made her

---

[3] In the writer's household account-book the following entries are made :—

Milk and cream	14	sous.
Two loaves	24	,,
Vegetables	6	,,
Salad	10	,,
Oil	2	,,
Vinegar	12	,,
Pepper	5	,,
Cheese	1	,,
Cider	18	,,
A fowl	8 10	,,

And in a note at the end, " Robespierre and Robert Lindet came to dinner."

tell me about their domestic life, it is exactly like ours, simple and frugal. Her brother had as little to do with the 10th of August as with the 2nd of September. He is as capable of being a party-leader as of catching hold of the moon. He is absent-minded like a thinker, cold and formal like a lawyer, but gentle as a lamb, and as sombre as Young. I see he has not our tender sensibility, but I believe he desires the good of the human race, though rather from justice than from love. For the rest, you need only see him face to face to be sure that nature never gave such attractive features to any but a noble mind. The younger Robespierre is more lively and more open, an excellent patriot, but of ordinary intelligence, and he has a petulant temper, which causes him to make too much noise and is unfavourable to the Mountain. David, the great painter, is your father's particular friend. He comes to all our parties. If he spoke as well as he paints, he would be Cicero and Brutus in one, for he has a truly Roman soul. Pache is assistant under Bournonville. He is a good man, knows how to ascend with modesty and descend with dignity, and wherever he can work for the public prosperity is in his right place. There is nothing so great as a great mind, and that is why a post more or less elevated does not signify, provided one can practise virtue and be useful to mankind.

LXXXVII.

PARIS, *February* 13, 1793.

The Brissotins, not being able to do any more direct harm, use every effort to prevent us from doing good, and they succeed only too well. Nothing is so urgent as the organization of our army. Dubois de Crancé's project appeared good to all the patriots, one would have thought it would be decreed without difficulty, excepting a few modifications of the less important articles. Not at all. After two long and stormy sittings only two things were obtained; first, the admission of the first article, and secondly the adoption of the principle of combining the soldiers of the line with the volunteers.

The dissensions which broke out at the beginning of the Convention will continue to the end. There is an age at which men change no more, and we have attained to that age. The wicked will not become good, nor the weak strong. Certain men of good faith who have gone astray, have renounced their errors, but they are few in number. Our greatest strength now lies in the force of public opinion, which must be maintained, extended, and fortified. If every one works at it with as much zeal and success as you do, our triumph will be prompt and sure. Adieu, dear child. Great dissatisfaction is felt at Bournonville's being chosen. I never expected anything good from the friend of Dumouriez. Great evils threaten us still, but I do not despair of seeing the end of them, and I am certain that the sacred cause of humanity will at last triumph everywhere.

LXXXVIII.

PARIS, *February* 19, 1793.

Monge was re-elected Minister of Marine, yesterday, by a great majority, which is a great pleasure to all true friends of the Republic. Our Convention and our Paris are as calm as a lake, and display the majesty of a great people who are filled with the sentiment of their rights and duties. Barbaroux and Rebequi are held in such horror at Marseilles, that some new deputies who are come from thence to the two clubs of the Jacobins and the Cordeliers have declared that their constituents were prepared to recall them at their first act of *incivisme*, and that the gates of the Republican city of Marseilles are for ever shut on those cowardly deserters of the good cause.

I like the application you make of the story of the tail of the horse of Sertorius. Preach confidence and hope, for we shall have a good Constitution, but such a great work requires to be polished and repolished more than once that it may not turn out a monstrosity like the other in which the different parties mutually destroyed each other. With patience and courage one succeeds in everything. I should like to be in a place like' yours, my dear

Commissioner of War, or your humble assistant. I
see so much good to be done, so many gentle virtues
to be exercised, that my heart, which always has the
largest share in all my actions, would find a thousand
delights there. How healthy and agreeable the
military prisons would be under my orders, how I
should soften by a tender generosity the punishments
I might be obliged to inflict, how carefully the
hospitals would be kept, and with what love of
humanity I should watch over them. The poor sick
people would be the objects of my constant solicitude,
and what joy it would be to provide shoes for those
valiant defenders of the country who are now going
bare-footed. I would give them my own garments
if I had no other means of clothing them, and how
attentively I would see that everything right and
just was done for them. Indeed, Commissioner, I
envy you your place, your youth, and your activity,
and all the means you possess of doing good. But
as you are my son, and I identify myself with you
in all you do, I acquire, through you, to whom I have
given life, a new and happy existence for myself. I
only gave you life, but you have given me the glory
and joy of having brought into the world a good
man, a faithful friend of humanity, a defender of the
weak poor, and the benefactor of all his fellow-
creatures when they require his help. That is your
natural destiny, and you will not disgrace it, I know.
When I compare the pleasure of a good action with
the greedy love of gold, I think mankind so fallen, so

degraded, that I pity them and am ashamed of them at the same time. Despise gold and riches, have but few wants, and avoid depending upon others. Keep your hands closed against the gifts that benevolence or even purity would bestow on you, and your ears against all dishonest insinuations. There are so many seductions of every kind, that one must be on one's guard against every one and everything.

There is my little sermon; I have written it almost in spite of myself. Adieu.

LXXXIX.

PARIS, *May*, 1793.

The ship is tempest tossed, and our pilots, the toys of human passion, instead of contending with the winds, instead of uniting their strength and skill, that they may bring it into harbour, are occupied in opposing each other. What a spectacle! Mariners fighting, while the waves are surging up around them to swallow them up! Oh! that Frenchmen, who are about to become the shame or the admiration of the universe, would at last assume that greatness of character which must secure our destinies. It is not among the people that this anarchy exists, it is among the constituted authorities: they set us an example of the most fatal dissension. The Corps Législatif, the Council of the Executive Power, the Commune of Paris, although composed of men who are on the side of the Revolution, are in such scandalous collision, that the aristocrats and the silly friends of royalty are eagerly calculating the profit they may make out of such lucky discord. *Divide to reign* is the motto of kings. *Fraternal union* will be that of peoples. The fasces loses all its strength by division. How generous those men would be who should say, "Let us all unite, that we may save all." If the zeal of one or other among us overpass the bounds of his power, let a fraternal warning recall him to moderation; but let us beware of bitterness and strife among ourselves, or we shall all perish. These petty private feuds, in the midst of the public calamities which we are threatened with, and which are actually upon us, make men appear as foolish as children who sport upon the brink of a precipice.

The Commune of Paris has saved France. The Corps Législatif was letting the country be destroyed, by a conspiracy which will astonish history by its vast extent, and its profound wickedness. The Corps Législatif itself has borne witness to this fact, by the decree in which it has said that the Commune of Paris *has deserved well of the country.* But a problem now presents itself for solution. May not the vigorous action which was so necessary be required again? Have not the Prussians and the Austrians sullied the territory of liberty by their presence? Are they not still on our frontiers? Are not the enemies within merely stunned for the moment? Are all the meshes of the plot broken? Ah, no; all their strength and wickedness might be restored in one moment. But you say, the Commune of Paris includes some scoundrels among its number. How foolish are some of your self-styled virtuous people, for you stigmatize by that name those who have saved you by their boldness and their firmness. It is only the wickedness of courts which has been sanctioned in all ages by vulgar prejudices. If our adversaries had succeeded in their designs, a million of Frenchmen would have perished by legal means, but as a parliament, or some other tribunal, would have formally arranged their bloody deaths, the humane sentiments of certain persons would not have been wounded. That one phrase, "it is the law," would have made everything legitimate. The safety of the people, which is the supreme law, has exacted, in the most terrible danger in which any nation could possibly be placed, sacrifices which have *not* been invested with legal forms, and the Commune, which favoured them, has made for itself bitter enemies of the false or the feeble friends of humanity. Roland and Servan, I appeal to you, because I believe you both to be high-souled men. You would not venture to order that an unjust thing should be done, to prevent a thing still more unjust. You would have, perhaps, already paid with your lives for the noble scruples that would have hindered you from preventing a thousand monstrous crimes by one illegal and cruel measure, which would have been justified by this plea alone : the safety of the people is the supreme law.

The constituted authorities ought now to be united in perfect harmony, by the unanimous and generous sacrifice of all those small passions and false scruples, above which true statesmen should rise. When the ferocious Austrians shall be driven out, when the perfidious autocrats shall be conquered, when all the snakes that strive to strangle us shall have been strangled, when the National Convention, like a young giant, shall enclose within its strong arms the genius of France, then the work of purifying the bed of the river through which has rolled the salutary flood that bore the vessel into port, may be undertaken. The safety of twenty-five millions of men, and perhaps the welfare of the universe is in question. Certain patriots form factions which struggle and contend with each other, and thus a party whose whole united strength is hardly sufficient to destroy the hydra of the counter revolution is divided. Among a firm and virtuous people Robespierre and Brissot would have sacrificed their individual differences, and sought only the general interest. Themistocles and Aristides, as well as two famous Romans, set them a splendid example. The legislator, the representative of a great people, the true man of the commonwealth, does not intrigue ; he has no creatures ; he does not procure places for any one ; he seeks con-

sideration for virtue only. For him individuals
have no existence, the general good absorbs all his
attention; and to that he sacrifices every passion.
His deadliest enemy, if he can but conduce to that,
he embraces, and bears him to the arena, for a
generous discussion of the good that is to be done.
They differ in opinion, but not in feeling; the desire
of both is for the happiness and prosperity of a
great people.

What a stain it is upon the names of those whom
we placed with pride among the number of our
liberators, that they have satellites who contend in
the temple of liberty. In an electoral assembly,
wherein resides the sovereignty of the people, it
is said, "Brissot's faction is having the best of it
to-day; to-morrow it will be Robespierre's turn."
Thus does an intriguing people make ready the
triumph of its enemies! Virtue alone could conquer them, and it is regarded as the weakest of
weapons. Cabals, coalitions, cliques, these are the
means that are employed. Brissot and Robespierre,
if you bring with you into the assembly that is
about to pronounce upon our destinies, your own
feuds and enmities, can we reckon you among the
number of the generous defenders of the people?
Save us, save yourselves! There is one open and
certain way, it is the union of patriots, and a magnanimous oblivion of all personalities. The pride
of a statesman ought to be noble and lofty, like his
functions. He is identified with the common weal,

and nothing that does not injure it should have the power to wound him. The self-love of a legislator ought to be hidden under an invulnerable shield. Rousseau said : " Gods are needed to govern men ;" and I say, only men are needed to govern the French, because that magnanimous people, taught by their misfortunes, and proud of having shaken off the fetters that held them in debasing slavery, need no longer anything but wise laws to secure their welfare. Justice, liberty, and equality, all that shall be built upon these sacred foundations must be immortal, like the Divinity whence those virtues emanate.[4]

[4] Here the correspondence comes to a close. Nothing is known of what passed between the mother and son afterwards, except by the following entry in the account-book :—

" *Arrested in the month of Thermidor* (10th August, 1794). *Jules arrived on the 22nd Thermidor, at ten o'clock. With all the pride of innocence, he went to give himself up to arrest, on the 23rd, between two and three o'clock.*"

THE END.

CPSIA information can be obtained
at www.ICGtesting.com
Printed in the USA
BVOW06s1426240817
493019BV00004B/16/P

9 781162 641225